PIPE FITTINGS

NIPPLES

PIPE LENGTHS UP TO 22 FT.

STRAIGHT COUPLING

REDUCING COUPLING

COUPLING

NUT

CAP

STRAIGHT TEE

REDUCING TEE

STREET TEE

STRAIGHT CROSS

REDUCING CROSS

90° ELBOW

90° ELBOW

90° ELBOW

45° ELBOW

REDUCING ELBOW

90° STREET ELBOW

45° STREET ELBOW

45° Y-BEND

REDUCING TEE

REDUCER

UNION (3 PARTS)

PLUG

BUSHING

CAP

RETURN BEND

90°

45°

UNION ELBOWS

STREET

UNION TEES

PLUG

45° ELBOW

TEE

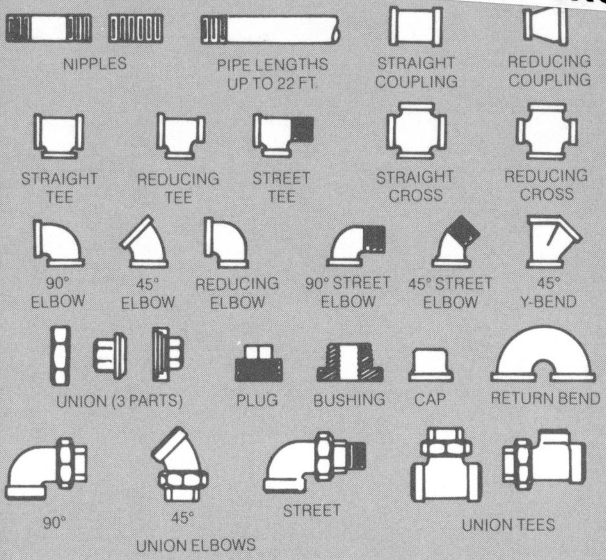

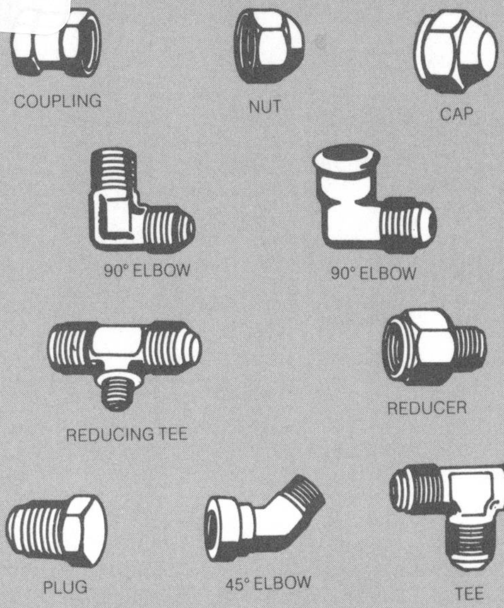

MEASURES OF CAPACITY

1 cup	=	8 fl oz
2 cups	=	1 pint
2 pints	=	1 quart
4 quarts	=	1 gallon
2 gallons	=	1 peck
4 pecks	=	1 bushel

STANDARD STEEL PIPE ((All Dimensions in inches)

Nominal Size	Outside Diameter	Inside Diameter	Nominal Size	Outside Diameter	Inside Diameter
⅛	0.405	0.269	1	1.315	1.049
¼	0.540	0.364	1¼	1.660	1.380
⅜	0.675	0.493	1½	1.900	1.610
½	0.840	0.622	2	2.375	2.067
¾	1.050	0.824	2½	2.875	2.469

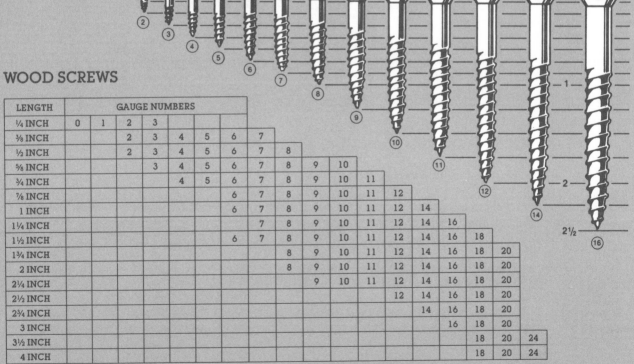

WOOD SCREWS

LENGTH	GAUGE NUMBERS													
¼ INCH	0	1	2	3										
⅜ INCH			2	3	4	5	6	7						
½ INCH			2	3	4	5	6	7	8					
⅝ INCH				3	4	5	6	7	8	9	10			
¾ INCH					4	5	6	7	8	9	10	11		
⅞ INCH							6	7	8	9	10	11	12	
1 INCH							6	7	8	9	10	11	12	14
1¼ INCH								7	8	9	10	11	12	14	16
1½ INCH							6	7	8	9	10	11	12	14	16	18
1¾ INCH									8	9	10	11	12	14	16	18	20
2 INCH									8	9	10	11	12	14	16	18	20
2¼ INCH										9	10	11	12	14	16	18	20
2½ INCH													12	14	16	18	20
2¾ INCH														14	16	18	20
3 INCH															16	18	20
3½ INCH																18	20	24
4 INCH																18	20	24

WHEN YOU BUY SCREWS, SPECIFY (1) LENGTH, (2) GAUGE NUMBER, (3) TYPE OF HEAD—FLAT, ROUND, OR OVAL, (4) MATERIAL—STEEL, BRASS, BRONZE, ETC., (5) FINISH—BRIGHT, STEEL BLUED, CADMIUM, NICKEL, OR CHROMIUM PLATED.

Popular Mechanics

do-it-yourself encyclopedia

The complete, illustrated home reference guide from the world's most authoritative source for today's how-to-do-it information.

Volume 5

CAMPING

to

CHILDREN'S FURNITURE

HEARST DIRECT BOOKS

NEW YORK

Acknowledgements

The Popular Mechanics Encyclopedia is published with the consent and cooperation of POPULAR MECHANICS Magazine.

For POPULAR MECHANICS Magazine:

Editor-in-Chief: *Joe Oldham*
Managing Editor: *Bill Hartford*
Special Features Editor: *Sheldon M. Gallager*
Automotive Editor: *Wade A. Hoyt, SAE*
Home and Shop Editor: *Steve Willson*
Electronics Editor: *Stephen A. Booth*
Boating, Outdoors and Travel Editor: *Timothy H. Cole*
Science Editor: *Dennis Eskow*

Popular Mechanics Encyclopedia

Project Director: *Boyd Griffin*
Manufacturing: *Ron Schoenfeld*
Assistant Editors: *Cynthia W. Lockhart, Peter McCann, Rosanna Petruccio*
Production Coordinator: *Peter McCann*

The staff of Popular Mechanics Encyclopedia is grateful to the following individuals and organizations:
Editor: *C. Edward Cavert*
Editor Emeritus: *Clifford B. Hicks*
Production: *Layla Productions*
Production Director: *Lori Stein*
Book Design: *The Bentwood Studio*
Art Director: *Jos. Trautwein*
Design Consultant: *Suzanne Bennett & Associates*
Illustrations: *AP Graphics, Evelyne Johnson Associates, Popular Mechanics Magazine, Vantage Art.*

Contributing Writers: Forest Belt, *Recorder repairs you can make*, page 569; Ivan Berger, *Snarled cassette tapes can be fixed*, page 572; Rosario Capotosto, *Surface boards the expert way*, page 563; *Pop-top desk*, page 615; Robert Charolais, *Snarled cassette tapes can be fixed*, page 572; Roy L. Clough Jr., *Tin-can space heater you can build*, page 520; William W. Conner, M.D., *Camping first aid*, page 530; Doug Dill, *Free-form candles molded in snow*, page 538; Max Farrell, *Coatrack for a child*, page 620; Warren H. Giles, *Heirloom cradle*, page 630; Charles R. Gretz, *It's a travelpod*, page 527; E.P. Haddon, *Camp-cruising by Kayak*, page 516; Len Hilts, *Ceiling tile installation*, page 574; Nick Karas, *Outfit for a wilderness canoe trip*, page 518; Laura Labarge, *Bunk bed with built-in chest*, page 628; Angus Laidlaw, *Survival gear for emergencies*, page 521; Wayne C. Leckey, *Candlemaking basics*, page 534; Paul Levine, *Playcubes—easy as 1, 2, 3*, page 632; Bill McKeown, *Sew your own camping gear*, page 523; Bernard Powell, *Antique ceiling beams*, page 582; Charles E. Rhine, *Tough cuts with your chain saw made easy*, page 586; Charles R. Self, *Carpentry*, page 551; Mort Schultz, *Charging system troubleshooting*, page 595; *Underhood cables and wiring*, page 602; *Alternator checks*, page 605; Ray Schoberg, *Hi-lo camper for your pickup*, page 525; Gary Stock, *Supercharge your car stereo*, page 544; Eugene Walters, *Car stereo speaker installation*, page 548; Willard and Elma Waltner, *Flamed candle stand*, page 531; *Holiday candle stand*, page 532; Paul Weissler, *Drive belt checks*, page 607; Harry Wicks, *Carpentry* (original material), page 551; Ralph S. Wilkes, *Caning made simple with prewoven rolls*, page 543; *Rolltop desk for your youngster*, page 621; Robert Wortham, *Chest in the Spanish style*, page 609; *Period pieces from stock molding*, page 612.

Picture Credits: Popular Mechanics Encyclopedia is grateful to the following for permission to reprint their photographs: Alpine Electronics of America, Inc., page 546 (bottom); Altec Lansing Corp., pages 545 (bottom) and 547; Analog & Digital Systems, Inc., page 546 (top); Philips Auto Audio, page 545 (top); Charles Self, page 560 (bottom), 561 (top left and right, and bottom right), 562 (bottom left and right); Jimmy Williams Photography, page 560 (top) and 561 (bottom left).

ISBN 0-87851-158-X

Library of Congress 85-81760

10 9 8 7 6 5 4

PRINTED IN THE UNITED STATES OF AMERICA

Contents

Camp-cruising by kayak

■ TODAY'S TOURING KAYAKS make it possible to copy safely the Eskimos' mode of travel. But for the long solo passages, you can do some customizing to improve on a good thing.

A little planning can make a kayak cockpit as shipshape as a submarine, with all essential safety and convenience gear stowed securely right at your fingertips. To plan placements aboard a 17-ft. folding kayak, the frame was assembled first without its hull covering. Fitting out hard-shell fiberglass kayaks can be done in much the same way.

You can install a nylon pocket to hold a nylon storm suit ready for instant use. Next to it is a canteen and a quart-size plastic soft drink bottle with a sipper tube. These are attached to the inside gunwale next to a knee, and held in place with ½-in. nylon straps like those used on backpacks. On the opposite gunwale, four small tackle boxes can be conveniently held in place with Velcro tabs. One drop of instant glue permanently attaches tabs on each box and matching tabs on the gunwale. No fisherman has ever

had lures within such easy reach. A single Velcro tab secures a small, liquid-filled compass to the kayak floor or to the deck for traveling off-shore or in foggy weather.

Because of a kayak's low center of gravity, particularly with air-filled side sponsons, there is little likelihood of capsizing it, but cargo bags, spotlights, sleeping bags and camera cases should be pretested for waterproof quality. You can then attach them to the kayak with ⅛-in. nylon lines to prevent loss. During an emergency, they can also provide added buoyancy. As a precaution, cargo bags may be lined with 3-mil plastic garbage bags tied off with rubber bands. Life preservers are required equipment.

Use an inflatable camera bag for flotation and cushioning. A pocket wind-velocity meter is another useful accessory.

Simplify photography aboard by anchoring your tripod in the mast step with a bungee cord. You can snap the camera with an air tube and bulb taped to the floor where you can push it with one foot. By prefocusing, you can record anything from scenics to fish being landed.

Customizing means fitting out and installing aids and equipment that are selected and positioned just right for you. Velcro tabs, shock and bungee elastic cord, oversize rubber bands slit from discarded inner tubes and nylon line are good for securing accessories. Nylon cord, like the surplus type used for static lines of parachutes, will lash gear in place, but they still untie easily, as a rule, when the knots get wet. Make good use of the line for lanyards on items like your bail scoop, searchlight and inflatable cushion, as well as cargo duffel. You can bring your bailer quickly to hand without leaving your seat with a pull on a color-coded line from your paddling position. The tie-lines would keep gear from floating away after an unlikely capsizing.

STOW CANTEENS, foul weather gear, anchor and fishing tackle where you can reach them easily.

DUFFEL BAGS, sleeping bag, spotlight and all "waterproof" and "floatable" items should be tested first and then secured to the boat.

FOR PHOTOS en route, mount a tripod with one leg through the mast socket and use a rubber tube with bulb extended to padder.

Outfit for a wilderness canoe trip

■ ONE MAN'S WILDERNESS is another man's backyard, and how to outfit or prepare for an excursion into either does and can differ considerably. There's no such thing as a standard outfitting list or technique because each trip will vary, based on the number in the party, the purpose of the trip, the kind of water to be traveled upon, the duration of the rides and the time of year the canoes go in the water.

The best approach might be to set up a theoretical trip and let you modify it according to your needs. The following list of materials, then, is for two men canoeing in semi-wilderness country—that is, they can drive to a putting-in place and take-out location. The river they run will have a few portages, maybe a lake or two, a little fast white water.

The early fall is good for trips into the bush because black flies and mosquitoes are usually at a low ebb, the weather is cooler and more pleasant than midsummer and the trees are likely to be in better color.

How to canoe is another story; this one is concerned with what you should bring along to make your trip successful. "What" will depend on the things you insist on having to be comfortable away from home. Tolerances differ with the individual.

Before you start a trip into the bush, you should make a checklist of what you think you'll need. If you've done it before, you'll realize that you have several checklists, probably these six: a basic outfitting list, a basic food list, a clothing list, a ditty-bag or personal list, a list of options concerned with the primary purpose of the trip if it is more than just canoeing, and a medical list that can be cut to one if you pick up a complete first-aid kit.

Believe it or not, all this equipment will fit nicely into a 16-foot canoe with enough room at the gunwales for ample safety. The small outboard motor is on the basic outfitting list for several reasons. In case of an emergency, you need it to get out in a hurry. If your trip doesn't end at a take-out place, it can get you upstream. It comes in handy for side trips up feeder streams and saves you time crossing lakes and on the open water.

Most equipment listed is self-explanatory. Unless you're taking along an extra large canoe, you can cut out some of the items. Remember, it all goes on your back each time there's a portage. The pop-type tent means you won't have to bring along poles or cut supports. An Adirondack packbasket is great because it's self-supporting and has canvas covers for use when it rains. Seat cushions are important to soften the load during the trip, serve as pillows and take the bumps out

BASIC OUTFITTING LIST

Tent, ground cloth	Scouring pads
Sleeping bag(s)	Dish towel
Air mattress	Poncho, rain suit
Catalytic stove	Life jacket(s)
Fuel: stove, lantern	Seat cushion(s)
Lantern mantles	Paddles (3)
Flashlight	Carrying yoke
Spare batteries, bulbs	Anchor, anchor line
Cooking stove	Bow lines
Cooking utensils	Tie-down lines
Eating utensils	Canoe patch kit
Cooking grate	Plastic tape
Packsack	Stovepipe wire
Ax, folding saw	Outboard motor, 1½-hp
Folding shovel	Motor bracket
Insect bomb	Motor fuel
Stick matches	Topographical maps
Liquid soap	Compass

BASIC FOOD LIST

Food lists depend on your personal taste, no pun intended. The following one covers only the basic staples, to which you can add the real bulk of the list—after planning meals, three a day, for every day you'll be away.

Shortening, flour	Evaporated milk
Margarine	Coffee, tea
Salt, pepper	Powdered chocolate
Sugar	Catsup
Dried milk	Mustard

CLOTHING LIST

This list will depend greatly on the time of year you make the trip and how often you like to change clothing.

Windbreaker	Handkerchiefs
Light ski jacket	Hat, with visor
Long-sleeved shirts	Gloves: cotton
Undershirts	Socks: wool, cotton
Underpants	Shoes: field, tennis
Trousers, shorts	Heavy belt

DITTY-BAG LIST

Toothpaste	Bath towel
Toothbrush	Sewing kit
Chapstick	Sunglasses
Pocket knife	Bar soap
Sheath knife (filet)	Paper towels
Insect repellent	Toilet tissue

FIRST-AID KIT

Adhesive tape	Merthiolate
Antiseptic ointment	Needle, tweezers
Adhesive bandages	Gauze pads, strips
Burn ointment	Salt tablets
Aspirin	Halazone tablets

of rocks and logs around the campfire at night, as well as being lifesaving devices. Even so, life jackets should also be in the canoe and worn when the water turns white or a long crossing of open water is at hand.

When canoeing in the rain, what to wear is a toss-up. Many older canoeists prefer a poncho; it gives them arm freedom and can be used to cover other gear when you're not under it. However, some of the new rainsuits are equally comfortable and can be stored in minimum space. The top also acts as a windbreaker on cool days.

If you don't take a fuel stove, then a fire grate is indispensable. Even if you have a stove, it's handy if the fuel should run out or you need an extra burner or two. It can be quickly set up between stones or logs.

If two paddles are good, then three are better to take on a trip. They have a way of breaking; the spare should always stay lashed inside the canoe in case you lose a paddle in a spill. It's too difficult to cut a new one in the bush that is as light or efficient as the extra one you bring along.

Spare batteries for a flashlight are fairly standard in most outfitting kits, but be sure to add a few bulbs. They do burn out and take such little space. Canoe repair kits—aluminum especially—can consist of heavy, reinforced tapes or tubes of liquid metal. A rubber patch kit for your sleeping bag or waders is also a good item to throw into the bag.

Use waterproof sleeping bags

Sleeping and clothing bags should be of waterproof plastic or rubberized cloth. There's nothing worse after a hard day on the paddle than a wet sleeping bag when it didn't even rain.

Electrician's plastic tape and stovepipe wire will have endless uses. A pair of pliers and a screwdriver should be in your tackle box. They're handy in so many unpredictable ways.

A Citizens Band radio is rather limited in range, with a maximum up to 20 miles. But sometimes that might be all the distance you need for an answer to your call for help. At night, the bounce can carry your plea halfway across the country. A portable radio is also a good idea. In some heavily canoed areas, radio stations have special programs for canoeists with messages from the outside world.

You might not find all the items on the lists helpful, or you might want to make additions to them to suit your own needs. The lists may have only given you a few ideas, but they're a place to start to build your own outfitting guide.

Tin-can space heater you can build

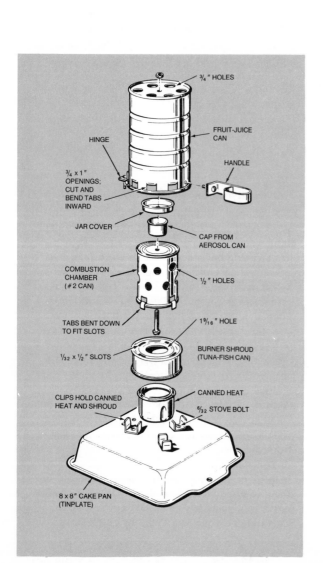

¾" HOLES

FRUIT-JUICE CAN

HINGE

¾ x 1" OPENINGS; CUT AND BEND TABS INWARD

HANDLE

JAR COVER

CAP FROM AEROSOL CAN

COMBUSTION CHAMBER (#2 CAN)

½" HOLES

TABS BENT DOWN TO FIT SLOTS

1⁹⁄₁₆" HOLE

¹⁄₃₂ x ½" SLOTS

BURNER SHROUD (TUNA-FISH CAN)

CLIPS HOLD CANNED HEAT AND SHROUD

CANNED HEAT

⁶⁄₃₂ STOVE BOLT

8 x 8" CAKE PAN (TINPLATE)

■ YOU'LL BE AMAZED at the blast of heat you get from a can of plain old Sterno when it is placed in this pint-size, inexpensive space heater. It is made from a collection of old tin cans and a pressed-steel cake pan which you probably have around the house. It is just the ticket for taking the chill from a boat cabin, tent or small trailer on those cold nights out in the woods.

The key features of the burner are a simple tuna-can shroud which insures a steady supply of air over the fuel to keep it from overheating and sputtering, and a burner pot which stabilizes the flame and insures that no unburned fumes escape. It's important that you follow the vent-hole sizes fairly closely. The cake-pan base never gets hot so it can be set down anywhere and you don't have to worry about it burning a tent or a table. One of the finer features is that the cake-pan base is also large enough that it is practically tip-proof.

The pull-apart drawing shows how the cans stack inside the hinged outer jacket which is a large fruit-juice can. The round holes can be neatly cut with a circle cutter, the square ones with an old wood chisel. In both cases, the metal should be backed up with a hardwood block to assure clean-cut holes. The clips on the base, plus the handle, are bent from short lengths of steel strapping.

Survival gear for emergencies

■ A HURRICANE, blizzard, power failure or other disaster can take away civilization all of a sudden, even today, and put us in a life-or-death situation. Emergencies often arise with little warning, but fortunately there are a number of new ways to prepare for them in advance. Products developed for everything from backpacking to space exploration are being adapted for house-

NEW HOME-AND-HIGHWAY aids: 1. Rescue unit combines 10 tools; one can cut car metal. 2. Pak-Kit contains shelter tent, flare, matches, cord, tape, blade. 3. Portable CB radio plugs into car cigarette lighter to transmit. 4. Combo strobe/fluorescent light gives illumination or red-flash warning. All of these items can be stowed in the trunk of your car to keep you prepared for an unexpected emergency on the road.

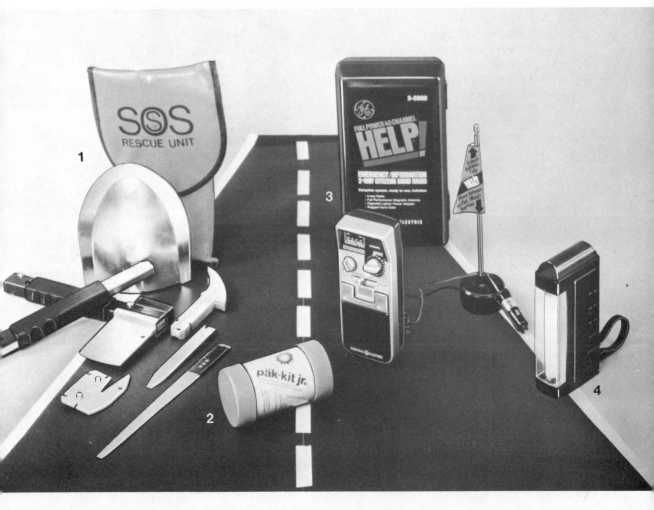

hold use, as homeowners store away supplies to see them through anything from a blackout to an earthquake.

Basic needs may include food, water, shelter and protection, communication and sanitary facilities. Most modern homes already have some survival gear on hand, although you don't call it that. Bathtubs, buckets and plastic garbage cans can be washed out and used for emergency water storage. Refrigerators and food freezers keep their cool much longer if packed full and kept closed. Add dry ice if you have time and if it's available. Warmth can be supplied with a fireplace, or camp heater. Even candles supply essential light and enough heat to warm some foods when the power goes out.

When it's cold outside, the important consideration is *keeping* warm; it's much easier to retain heat than to try to rewarm a home. The new outdoor sporting equipment—ski clothes, down vests, thermal underwear, insulated boots, battery-heated socks and mittens—will all help. Recently developed synthetics insulate clothing to help retain heat, and metalized space blankets also retard heat loss. An outdoorsman's snow-country clothing makes for welcome indoor wear when the heat goes off.

Don't overlook your car outside, either, when electricity fails at home. As long as it isn't parked in a closed garage and the exhaust isn't blocked, you can sit in your car to warm up with the engine running, and listen to the car radio for disaster information. Better still, you can communicate your problems if you have a CB radio transmitter.

STORAGE SUPPLIES include: 1. Dehydrated bulk foods. 2. A 12/115/220-volt refrigerator.
3. Canned milk. 4. Packaged meals. 5. Mini-lantern.
6. Backpack stove. 7. Waterproof matches and oversize candles. 8. Super Straw for water purification treatment.

On the road

A well-stocked car trunk normally will have tire and motor-repair tools. In addition, consider the following: a tow cable and a coil of rope plus a lever-type winch, flares, reflectors, flashlight and hand spotlight, jumper cables, small camp stove, mess kit, ice chest with dehydrated food, waterproof matches and candles stowed inside, ground cloth, space blanket and army blanket, duct tape and wire, coveralls and rain gear, work gloves, first-aid kit, hatchet, and possibly, in cold climates, a sleeping bag. This may seem like an extensive list, but all the items should fit into an ice chest and duffle bag. Fortunately, weight isn't the problem it might be for a backpacker. In warm weather, a canteen, water jug, 12-volt portable refrigerator and possibly even a snake-bite kit might be added.

Sew your own camping gear

SEW-IT-YOURSELF Aspen jacket comes in kit form. A few hours' work converts kit pieces into a quality down-filled coat.

■ HOW WOULD YOU like a 50-percent discount on camping gear that you need? Not cheap equipment, either, but the very best obtainable—finely made and probably better than any you could order anywhere.

Nor is your choice limited to a handwoven belt or watch band. Look over the list below and see if there isn't an item—or, more likely, many—that you wish you had:

Down-filled sleeping bag
Bag liner
Bivouac cover
Down jacket
Parka
Ski coat
Down vest
Down sweater
Down pants
Gaiters
Poncho
Booties
Overboots
Chaps
Rain gear
Tent
Stuff sack and backpack
Bike bag

Many of these come in assorted sizes, types and colors, while the variety of items offered is growing all the time.

At first glance, the price tag for a sleeping-bag kit or tent kit can seem steep, especially since you still have to put it together. But if you don't enjoy working with your hands, you probably wouldn't take up camping, and the kit manufacturers have found their customers already know about but don't want the flimsy cutrate items from some surplus outlets. For example, if you buy a sleeping-bag kit which is rated −20° F. and then add the optional "expedition down fill" for even more insulation, it's obvious you want the best. Or perhaps you select a model which weighs about five and a half pounds. You can sew the special full-length foam pad right into the down bag, where it is always ready for use.

Because you do the sewing, you can be sure that no one took shortcuts on inside seams that don't show, and you can also double-stitch or lock-stitch spots where you know from experience a zipper can tear or a D-ring pull loose when you're miles from nowhere. Basic sewing experience is helpful, though not essential, and these kits could be sewn by hand rather than machine if you had a lot of time.

Even after years of sewing, you may not be

used to edge-seared fabric, but the instructions make it easy. You carefully pass a flame along the edge of the ripstop nylon without touching it. The heat seals the edge so that it will never unravel during wear, washing or cleaning. It is easy to see why in normal factory assembly there's not time to spare for refinements such as this.

To test kit instructions and materials, and because they looked great, we first selected down booties and overboots available in blue, green, or orange. Both came with all the materials—thread, elastic, cord and laces—plus illustrated instructions so explicit that someone who had never sewn before could have worked them out.

Many of the products come in a variety of sizes, ranging down to clothing for children and pack carriers for babies. Some of the sleeping bags start with 42-inch lengths, and then can later be extended with 12-inch sections as the youngster grows. Provided in small plastic packs is the down you will use to fill the insulated clothing and bags. This, we found, is a neat and easy way to handle the very fluffy feathers.

And even if you have no plans for camping or cool-weather sports, the kit makers' catalogs deserve study for their versatile bargain travel packs and bags. We test-constructed kits from each, and found them uniformly well designed. They were complete with all necessary parts, and with instructions that told both the how, and reassuringly, the why of each succeeding step.

Cross-country and downhill skiers, hunters, bicyclists and travelers using almost any other means of getting around are likely to find kits designed especially for them.

TURNING PARTS into a pack took an evening, following kit's complete instructions and using all the comprehensive enclosures.

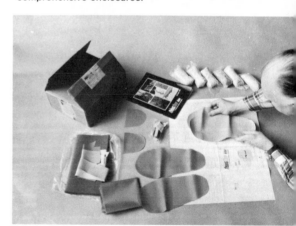

Fabrics, goose down packs and thread were in the boot and bootie kits

Hi-lo camper for your pickup

■ DON'T CONFUSE a camper shell with a standard pickup camper. The shell bolts directly to the top flange of your pickup box, and unlike a camper, it has no lower sidewalls or floor. Ultralight, it can usually be lifted on or off the truck without the aid of winches or jacks.

The two-part shell detailed here has several advantages over commercial shells. When you buy a shell, you have to choose between a low-profile model roughly the same height as your truck cab and a high-rise style which offers standup headroom.

The higher shells are more comfortable to live in, but they are also bulkier and offer greater wind resistance. Low shells are considerably more cramped. However, they're more compact, lighter and generally handier for year-round utility shelter for your pickup box.

With this two-part shell, you can choose the height to suit the job. The shell itself is a standard low-ceiling design. However, sandwich in the extender between the shell and truck box and you have a stand-up shell. You can also use the extender alone to increase the height of your pickup box for hauling bulky loads. Temporary hooks screwed into the top plate will provide anchorage to lash down the load or secure a tarp.

Before starting construction, it's a good idea to have all the materials and fittings on hand so they can be measured exactly. Window openings, for example, shouldn't be cut until you have the windows available to use as a cutting pattern. This way you'll be assured of a perfect fit.

You may have a problem finding some of these parts through local sources. If so, you can order the windows, aluminum skin, metal roof and moldings from camping supply dealers.

From the drawings, you should have no trouble visualizing the general construction of the shell and extender. Both are framed with 2x2s and faced with aluminum skin on the outside and plywood paneling on the inside. Naturally, dimensions must be tailored to suit your pickup.

While you can leave the walls hollow, it costs very little to insulate them with batts of fiberglass. This will make the shell cooler in summer and warmer in cold weather. It's well worth the slight extra cost.

If you want to work indoors, the sides, front and back can be partially finished in your workshop and then assembled later outdoors. Construct the framing and attach the inside paneling. Before doing the roof, however, check the dimensions against those of your shop door to make sure you'll be able to get it out.

Take all length and width measurements from the pickup box itself. Height is a matter of taste, but remember that the roof should protrude slightly above the cab if you plan to haul loads on top.

PLYWOOD GUSSETS on the side panels give curve to the roofline and anchor the brackets that support a pair of carrier bars as sturdy as necessary.

FIBERGLASS INSULATION is well worth the slight added expense. Note that the front 2x2 has been rounded off to conform to the shape of the plywood gusset.

ROOF VENT FRAMING should be installed now, even though you may not put one in immediately. Drill tiny locator holes in the corners for cutting opening later.

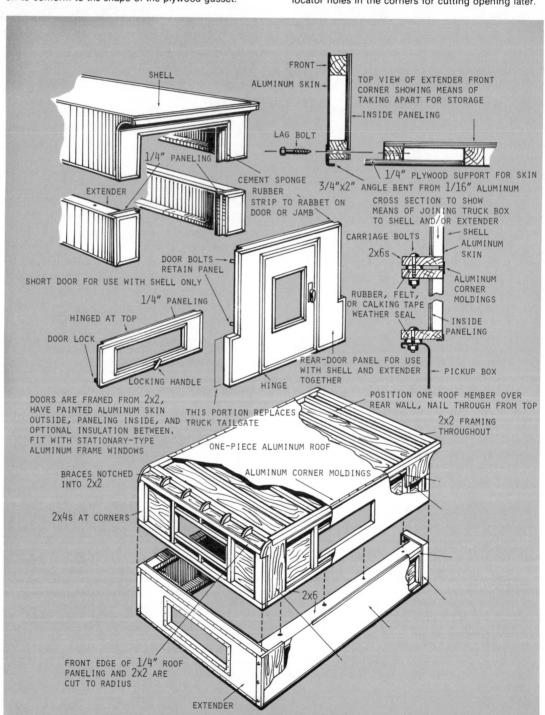

SHELL

FRONT

ALUMINUM SKIN

TOP VIEW OF EXTENDER FRONT CORNER SHOWING MEANS OF TAKING APART FOR STORAGE

INSIDE PANELING

LAG BOLT

1/4" PLYWOOD SUPPORT FOR SKIN

1/4" PANELING

EXTENDER

CEMENT SPONGE RUBBER

3/4"x2" ANGLE BENT FROM 1/16" ALUMINUM

STRIP TO RABBET ON DOOR OR JAMB

CROSS SECTION TO SHOW MEANS OF JOINING TRUCK BOX TO SHELL AND/OR EXTENDER

CARRIAGE BOLTS

SHELL

2x6s

ALUMINUM SKIN

DOOR BOLTS RETAIN PANEL

ALUMINUM CORNER MOLDINGS

SHORT DOOR FOR USE WITH SHELL ONLY

RUBBER, FELT, OR CALKING TAPE WEATHER SEAL

1/4" PANELING

INSIDE PANELING

HINGED AT TOP

DOOR LOCK

REAR-DOOR PANEL FOR USE WITH SHELL AND EXTENDER TOGETHER

PICKUP BOX

LOCKING HANDLE

HINGE

POSITION ONE ROOF MEMBER OVER REAR WALL, NAIL THROUGH FROM TOP

DOORS ARE FRAMED FROM 2x2, HAVE PAINTED ALUMINUM SKIN OUTSIDE, PANELING INSIDE, AND OPTIONAL INSULATION BETWEEN, FIT WITH STATIONARY-TYPE ALUMINUM FRAME WINDOWS

THIS PORTION REPLACES TRUCK TAILGATE

2x2 FRAMING THROUGHOUT

ONE-PIECE ALUMINUM ROOF

ALUMINUM CORNER MOLDINGS

BRACES NOTCHED INTO 2x2

2x4s AT CORNERS

2x6

FRONT EDGE OF 1/4" ROOF PANELING AND 2x2 ARE CUT TO RADIUS

EXTENDER

It's a travelpod

■ IF THE CAMPING BUG hasn't had his stinger into you yet, watch out! Here's just the rig that could give you the fever. It's the perfect answer to family camping in a car.

What's so great about it? Imagine being able to take off with a king-size, cartop luggage carrier that packs a whopping 36 cubic feet of waterproof tote space!

Imagine having an overnight sleeper when you arrive that's as easy to set up as an umbrella!

Imagine being able to take along your own boat for a day of trolling a quiet stream!

All this is possible with this all-in-one travelpod that has been designed, built, and tested with 300 pounds of camping gear. It turned out to be the most versatile and most functional camper on the road. What's more, you have the whole car to yourself since everything can be stowed topside.

The Pod is designed to mount on regular steel luggage bars that rest on the wagontop and clip to the rain gutters. Access to the sleeper is by an aluminum boat ladder that stows on the underside of the sliding lid. To open the Pod on the road, you simply slide back its lid; it has handles to lift it off. Contents are safe from rain by virtue of a tongue-and-groove waterproof track and are secured from theft by foot-locker-type trunk latches and a padlock.

One person can set up the Pod in minutes for sleeping. It's draftproof and you'll have no fear that the kids will fall out. Nylon-net windows ventilate the tent and, by design, the overhang of the roof provides adequate sun and rain protection. The tent rolls in a bundle only 8 in. in diameter by 6 ft. long and weighs 15 lbs.

The broad, flat bottom allows the Pod to be a stable, minimum-draft boat. A small electric trolling motor is ideal to propel it and will run all day on a fully charged car battery. There's plenty of shade under the nose cone for an ice cooler, even a mini-TV set.

On the road, the Pod is less than 2 ft. high and is designed to present minimum resistance to the wind. Yet it pops into instant service.

For the most part, the Pod and its lid are made of ¼-in. marine plywood. Members that form the tongue-and-groove tracks are of solid stock.

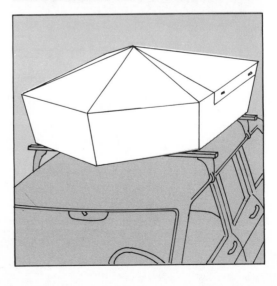

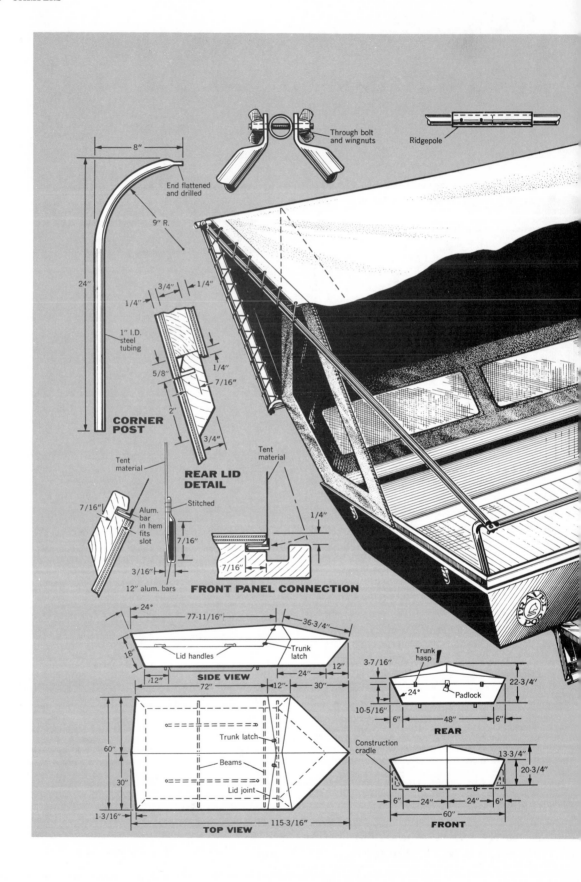

Through bolt and wingnuts

Ridgepole

8″

End flattened and drilled

9″ R.

24″

1″ I.D. steel tubing

3/4″   1/4″

1/4″

5/8″   1/4″

7/16″

2″

3/4″

CORNER POST

REAR LID DETAIL

Tent material

Tent material

1/4″

7/16″

Alum. bar in hem fits slot

Stitched

7/16″

3/16″

7/16″

12″ alum. bars

FRONT PANEL CONNECTION

24°

77-11/16″

36-3/4″

Lid handles

Trunk latch

18″

Trunk hasp

3-7/16″

Padlock

24°

22-3/4″

SIDE VIEW

12″

72″

12″

24″

12″

30″

10-5/16″

6″   48″   6″

REAR

60″

Trunk latch

Beams

Lid joint

Construction cradle

13-3/4″

20-3/4″

30″

1-3/16″

115-3/16″

TOP VIEW

6″   24″   24″   6″

60″

FRONT

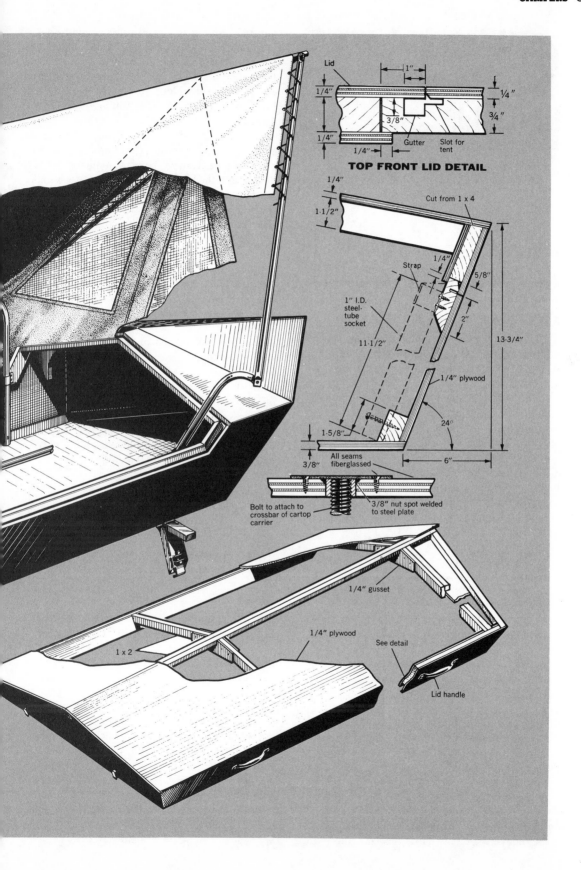

Lid

1/4″

1″

1/4″

3/4″

3/8″

1/4″

1/4″

Gutter

Slot for tent

TOP FRONT LID DETAIL

1/4″

1·1/2″

Cut from 1 x 4

1/4″

Strap

5/8″

1″ I.D. steel-tube socket

2″

11·1/2″

13-3/4″

1/4″ plywood

24°

1·5/8″

6″

3/8″

All seams fiberglassed

Bolt to attach to crossbar of cartop carrier

3/8″ nut spot welded to steel plate

1/4″ gusset

1/4″ plywood

See detail

1 x 2

Lid handle

Camping first aid

■ VACATIONERS ARE FREQUENTLY far from medical help when an injury occurs—so it's important to know alternate first-aid methods for some common ills:

Fishhook penetration

The old recommended method for removing a fishhook was to force the point out through the skin and cut off the eye so it would pass through the hole thus made.

An equally good, and often less damaging to the victim, method employs an 18-inch length of string which is looped around the bend of the hook and held slack. With your other hand grasp the eye of the hook and press the shank down in the direction of the point. At the same time the shank is depressed, give the string a sharp jerk— and out snaps the hook. A little disinfectant over the wound, and you're ready to bait up again.

Snake bites

America has only four types of truly venomous snakes: rattlesnake, copperhead, moccasin and coral snake. Other snakes may bite when alarmed, but they lack venom and fangs.

A new method used by doctors in handling snake bites is to remove a patch of skin from the site of the bite about the size of a half dollar, along with the underlying tissue. The venom usually collects here in large quantities, and removing the tissue rids the victim of most danger. The limb is then treated with antivenom injected into an artery, and a new piece of skin is later placed over the wound. Most of this is obviously best left to the doctor. What, then, can be done in the way of first aid?

First, allow the victim to expend as little energy as possible. This helps slow down circulation and delays absorption into the system. Second, apply a snug tourniquet about two inches above the bite. That is, between the bite and the heart. It is a good rule of thumb that if you cannot easily push your finger under the tourniquet, it is too tight. A greater danger results from applying it too tightly than too loosely; a leg can be lost if the blood supply is cut off for too long. Third, transport the victim to a hospital or a doctor.

Note that no mention is made of cutting or sucking on the bite area! However, if the accident occurs where it may take many hours to reach a doctor, and the bite was from a moccasin, a snake whose venom is particularly destructive to injected tissue, your first aid should be more extensive. The area of the bite should be cut out. All that is necessary is a clean, sharp knife. The venom itself provides good anesthesia. Make a circular incision about two inches in diameter with the fang marks in the center. Cut deep enough to include the fat that lies under the skin. The venom may have blackened the fat, and by picking out all of the blackened tissue visible, you can remove much of the stored venom. A careful cleaning of the wound with a good disinfectant before and after the operation and a sterile or clean pressure-dressing will suffice to ward off infection until you get medical help.

More complications can arise from an infected wound than from the snake bite itself! So avoid making any cuts in the skin unless a long delay in reaching the doctor is unavoidable.

Bleeding

Bleeding from any cause can usually be treated most effectively by applying firm pressure with a clean cloth directly on the wound. Forget tourniquets and pressure points unless the bleeding is from a severed limb.

Burns

Perhaps the most common vacation mishap is a burn—sunburn, campfire burn, lantern burn and others. The treatment is similar for all. The prime consideration is to stop tissue damage as quickly as possible, and the best counteractant for heat is cold. So plunge the burned area into cold water immediately—a cold stream, a pail of drinking water, or over the side of a boat. Hold it in the water until the pain subsides. Many otherwise serious burns treated in this simple manner can be reduced to not much more than a moderate sunburn. A clean and dry dressing or a small amount of antibiotic ointment can then be used to cover the area. Avoid the age-old "goo treatment" or butter, baking soda and the like. These applications often make matters worse.

■ THIS UNIQUE candle stand begins as a 3½x3½x4-in. redwood cube. Turn the wells for the three sizes of candles in the top plane of the cube, following the dimensions given. Trace the carving designs on the four sides of the cube so that like designs are on sides opposite each other.

Before flaming the block, recess the background ⅛ in. deep with carving burrs in a drill press. Clamp a piece of wood to the drill-press table to make the straight outer cuts, and clean out the rest of the wood freehand. With the cube clamped in a vise, use a propane torch at low flame and pass it back and forth over the work so the tip just touches the wood to char it lightly.

If the wood should catch fire, blow it out. If necessary, remove heavy charring from the cube with a wire brush. Move the brush with the grain, then rub the block with a soft cloth and apply two coats of a satin-finish clear lacquer.

Flamed candle stand

BLOCK IS MOUNTED in four-jaw lathe chuck and wells are turned in top for three sizes of candles.

BACKGROUND OF DESIGN is carved freehand to a depth of ⅛ in. with a burr cutter in the drill press.

CARVED PATTERNS

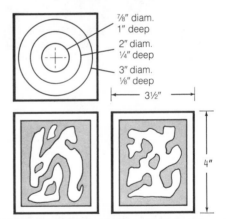

⅞" diam. 1" deep
2" diam. ¼" deep
3" diam. ⅛" deep
3½"
4"

BOARD IS CLAMPED to a drill-press table for a fence to guide the block when you make straight burr cuts.

Holiday candle stand

■ DESIGNED TO HOLD jumbo candles up to 3 in. in diameter, this attractive candle stand makes a festive centerpiece for the Christmas holidays.

First make a full-size pattern for one of the arms and trace it on your wood. If you have a bandsaw, you can saw all six arms at one time by tacking the ½-in. stock together in the waste areas. A router with a corner-rounding bit makes quick work of rounding the edges of the arms, but you also can do it with a contour sander or a sanding drum in the drill press. If you have to do

it by hand, start with a coarse sandpaper and finish with fine.

The candle cap is lathe-turned from a ¾-in.-thick disc and recessed ⅛ in. Again, if you don't have a lathe, it can be built up from three jig-sawed discs.

If you have used open-grain wood such as mahogany or walnut, apply paste wood filler before assembling the parts. Glue and nails are used to attach the arms to the cup. Add two arms at a time, one opposite the other, and clamp. Complete with self-rubbing clear satin finish.

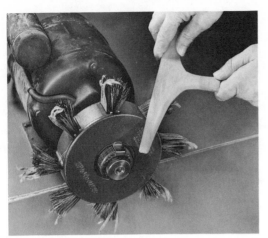

AFTER SAWING OUT the arms, all edges are rounded with a contour sander or sanding block.

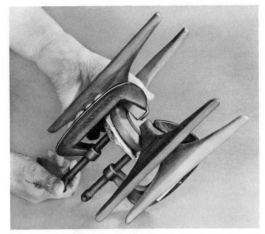

THEN THE ARMS are glued and nailed to the bottom of the candle cup and clamped until the glue dries.

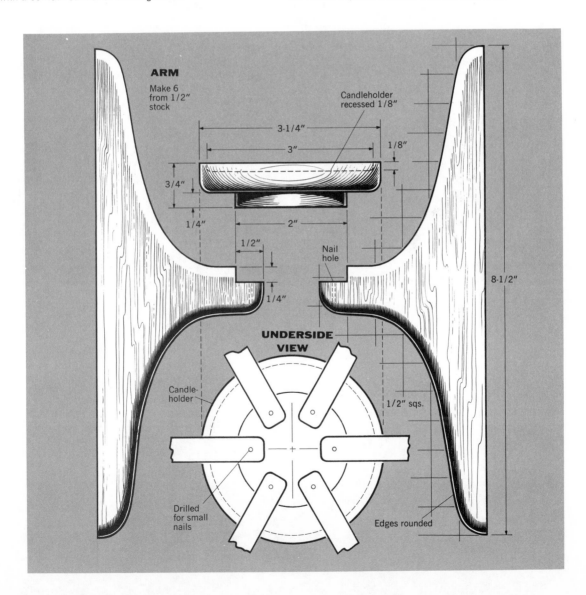

ARM

Make 6 from 1/2" stock

Candleholder recessed 1/8"

3-1/4"

3"

1/8"

3/4"

2"

1/4"

1/2"

Nail hole

1/4"

8-1/2"

UNDERSIDE VIEW

Candle-holder

1/2" sqs.

Drilled for small nails

Edges rounded

Candlemaking basics

■ FANCY CANDLES make perfect Christmas gifts—they're colorful, decorative and useful; they symbolize Christmas, and they're gifts that everyone likes to receive.

What's more, they are homemade gifts that don't look homemade. Cast in fancy reusable molds, they have a ready-made, store-bought look that compares with candles which bring fancy prices in gift shops. Yet they cost pennies to make and anyone can make them. The

MELT WAX in a double boiler, never over direct heat. Melted wax should be no hotter than 175-185°F.

ADD COLORING after wax is completely melted. Stir and allow the coloring to dissolve thoroughly.

"tools" required are common household items for the most part, and hobby stores provide a ready source for the molds, wax, wicking, scent, coloring and other items. And once you're hooked by this fascinating hobby, you'll soon be making your own molds from Silastic RTV compounds. You'll be creating such unique forms as ice candles, whipped-wax candles, sand candles and others. You'll be decorating them in gold, spray painting them in pearl and iridescent tones and adding glitter to make them sparkle. There are many good books on candlemaking which take you beyond the basic steps explained here.

Kinds of molds

Candles can be cast in countless sizes and shapes, and in several kinds of molds. Flexible,

rubberlike stretch molds are one-piece molds which you remove from the finished candle by pulling them off like rubber gloves—inside out. Such molds, like others, can be used over and over.

Vacuum-formed plastic molds are two-part molds of matching halves that are self-aligning but must be sealed at the edges with masking tape.

Metal candle molds, straight and tapered, are available up to 18 in. tall. Handsome one, two and three-wick candles, round, triangular and star-shaped, can be cast in metal molds.

Wax, wick, coloring and scent

Candle wax comes in slab and granular form, and can be melted and remelted again and again.

Wicking comes in spools of 100 and 300 ft.,

TWO-PIECE plastic molds consist of matching halves bound and sealed at the edges with masking tape.

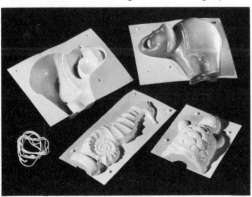

ONE-PIECE stretch molds are flexible. To remove from the candle, you pull them off like a rubber glove.

also in 6 and 12-ft. lengths, braided or cored. Braided wicking is specially made for use with metal molds, whereas core wicking is for non-metal molds.

Coloring is sold in square, granular, powder and stick form. It's added to the melted wax before pouring and allowed to dissolve completely. It comes in all colors of the rainbow, and color is controlled by the amount that's added to the wax. Regular coloring-book crayons also can be used to color candle wax.

Similarly you can add fragrance to your candles. Available in some 17 different scents, it's added to the melted wax after the color and just before pouring. A ¼-oz. bottle will scent 5 lbs. of wax.

Melting the wax

Candle wax is melted in a double boiler, never over direct heat. A fruit-juice can, or a 1-lb. coffee can, fitted with a suitable handle and pinched at the rim to form a pouring lip, makes a good ladle in which to melt wax. It's best to have a couple of such ladles at hand so you can have two double boilers going at one time. Bring the water in your outer vessel to a slow boil, then turn the heat down to a medium simmer. Wax should be about 175–185°F., no hotter. You can test it with a candy thermometer.

Setting up your mold

One of the best ways to support a rubber stretch mold is to rest it in an inverted cardboard paint-bucket liner. A hole is cut in the bottom to accommodate the mold, and the mold is suspended in the hole. In the case of two-piece plastic molds, the two halves are sealed around the edges with masking tape (after the wick is in place, of course) and the mold is supported vertically. A simple way to do this is to use a small vise which clamps over the edge of a table, and secure the mold in it.

Metal molds are no problem: they're free-standing and can't tip over.

Inserting the wick

In most cases, depending upon the particular mold, the wick is placed in the center and supported at the top. When working with rubber molds, the wick can be held with a pencil placed across the top. In the case of two-part plastic molds, the wick is held in place with tabs of masking tape. Here the wick is cut long enough to stick out both ends of the mold and the ends taped. When working with metal molds, the wick is attached to the bottom of the mold and wound around a rod bridging the top. In each case the wick is first dipped in melted wax and allowed to cool before it is centered in the mold. Predipping the wick will make it burn better.

Melted wax is hot so take care in pouring it into your mold. Also, avoid getting any water in the wax since it will cause bubbles in the finished candle. Fill the mold almost to the top and let stand. As it cools, wax shrinks, so when it starts to get a crust, poke a hole through the hardened wax and add more melted wax to bring it level. You may have to do this several times as the wax continues to shrink and form air pockets. It requires about three hours for the wax to harden. To cure, place the mold overnight in a refrigerator. Chilling will also give added shine to the wax.

Tilting the mold while filling it, as you can with metal molds, and gradually bringing the mold upright as you pour helps prevent the wax from becoming cloudy due to excessive air bubbles.

Removing candle from mold

A flexible mold is removed from the candle much the same way as pulling a rubber glove from the hand; it's actually turned inside out. Dusting the outside of the mold with talcum will keep it from sticking to itself.

To open a two-part mold the tape is peeled from the edges and the halves gently pulled free. If they stick, hold the mold under hot water for a few seconds. Spraying the mold beforehand with silicone or coating with cooking oil will ensure easy release. To remove a candle from a metal mold you simply turn the mold upside down and tap the bottom lightly. A knife can be used to pare and smooth any unwanted ridges.

Finishing off the bottom of candles so they sit level can be done in two ways. You can shave off the wax with a rasplike tool called Surform, or you can rub the candle over the bottom of a pan placed over low heat on your rangetop.

Novelty candles in the form of frogs, turtles, owls, seahorses, snowmen, mushrooms and the like are especially fun to make, as are candles that float. New for a garden pool or romantic table centerpiece, lighted floating candles are fascinating to watch with their ever-changing reflections. The candles resemble lily pads. They are cast in flexible molds while they rest in pans of water. You release the finished candle from its mold by gently *pulling* (not pushing) each of the petal "separators" *away* from the core.

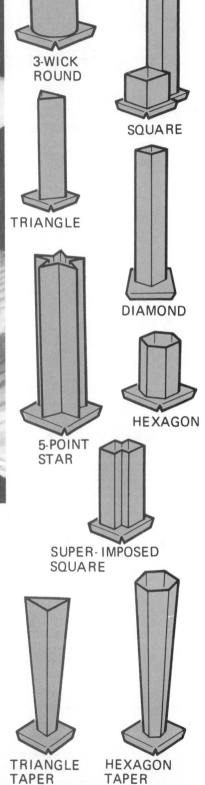

A SMALL VISE and spring clamps are handy for holding together the halves of a large plastic mold. A notched brace helps hold it steady for pouring.

3-WICK ROUND

SQUARE

TRIANGLE

DIAMOND

HEXAGON

5-POINT STAR

SUPER-IMPOSED SQUARE

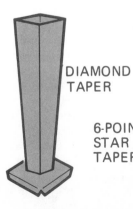

ROUND TAPER

PYRAMID

DIAMOND TAPER

6-POINT STAR TAPER

TRIANGLE TAPER

HEXAGON TAPER

Free-form candles molded in snow

UNIQUE CANDLES are created by pouring wax into a snow "mold." Resulting designs are as varied as snowflakes.

■ SNOW CAN BE the mold you use to create candles that take on a frosty appearance, yet provide a warm glow for winter nights. Hot wax melts and changes its snow molds as it solidifies, producing unusual textures and shapes. And with snow molds, no two candles are ever alike.

Snow candles are made with your favorite brands of candle wax, colors, scents and wicks. Snow becomes the mold. The process is like making sand candles except that the snow molds are not as predictable as sand and can result in pleasant surprises for the candlemaker.

If you live in snow country you can melt the wax in the normal fashion on your home stove. If you have to travel to the snow, a campstove makes a fine source of heat. In either case, use a double boiler, never direct heat.

Start making your molds in the snow while the wax is melting. Simply create a depression that wax can be poured into. Dangle a wick into the depression from a stick placed across its rim; the wick should be coated with melted wax and allowed to dry thoroughly before being placed in the mold. Wire-core wicks seem to work best.

There are two basic types of snow candles. The "upside down" candle is made by sculpting a design in the bottom of your depression in the snow. After the wax is poured and set, the candle is removed and turned upside down for use.

More unpredictable designs happen with the two-pour candle. After one pour has solidified completely, more wax, usually of a second color, is poured into the mold. Results can be surprising. Instead of filling the mold to the top, the second pour will run to the bottom of the mold and harden under the first, making its own design. This candle is not inverted, but used in the position in which it is formed. Usually some wax must be removed from the bottom to make it sit flat; use a hot knife and be careful not to break off delicate parts. Sometimes the second pour will go deeper than the wick and another must be inserted; use a heated icepick to make a hole, place the new wick and pour melted wax around it.

It takes about an hour for wax to harden enough for removal from the snow. Be very careful when digging out the candle—parts may spread far from the original mold and can easily be broken.

Snow characteristics will affect candles. Try molds made in new or soft snow, both packed and unpacked. Crusty or melting snow makes interesting but generally more predictably shaped candles.

Caning a chair

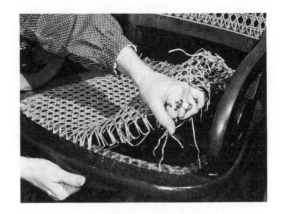

■ SEATS AND BACKS of woven cane have been used in fine furniture for several centuries. They look good, they're durable, and they're comfortable to sit on. But in time, the cane becomes worn and breaks, and when this happens there is little you can do to repair it. Your only option is to install new cane.

Because the pattern of the woven cane looks intricate, most people assume that the weaving is a job for experts only. Actually, cane weaving is a fairly simple operation, requiring no special tools, and no great skill or strength. You need only the materials, available from a dozen or more good mail-order sources, and the patience to follow a prescribed series of steps.

Cane is the outer bark of the rattan palm found in India, China, Ceylon and Malaysia. It is cut into strips varying in width from 1/16- to 3/16-in., and bundled into hanks of 1000 feet, with individual strips in the hank ranging up to 18 feet in length. You can also buy 500-foot hanks.

You pay a small premium for selected cane of

CANE WEAVING requires no special tools, great strength or skill. Caning a chair begins by removing the old cane (top right). Pegs help hold the first course as it is woven back and forth (right). The second course (lower left) is woven across the chair. A final diagonal course of cane goes over and under, providing the unique cane pattern (lower right). Complete do-it-yourself instructions are on the pages that follow.

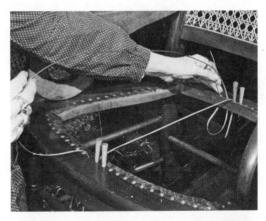

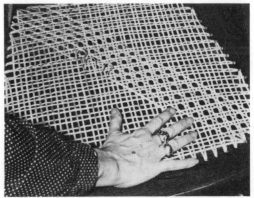

higher quality, and an additional premium for select long cane, where every strip in the hank is more than 12 feet long.

Since 1,000 feet will cane an area of about 4 square feet (24 by 24 inches), a hank will serve three to four average chairs.

Good-quality cane is important and the investment in "select" cane is wise. Poor cane doesn't weave easily because of rough spots. Good cane is smooth and the "eye"—a small lump on the cane from which the leaf grew—is smooth and unbroken.

The materials to cane a chair include the regular weaving cane and binding cane, and the only tools you need are a caning awl and caning pegs. Binding cane is simply strands of cane two sizes wider than the weaving cane, and every hank comes with enough binding cane included in it to take care of several seats.

Caning pegs are tapered hardwood pegs which are pushed into the cane holes in the chair rail to hold the cane in place as you weave. However, you don't even have to buy these, since golf tees work quite well in this job. A caning awl can be any long, thin prod, and is used to push the cane through the holes, but if you already have an ice pick, it will serve just as well.

Cane comes in six widths, and the width you order is determined by the size of the holes in the chair rail. If you have some of the old cane, measure its width. If not, measure the hole size. Consult the chart on this page, and order your cane by both name and hole size.

There is some variation in cane terminology from supplier to supplier. Some call the narrowest strip "carriage" instead of superfine. Your best bet is to send for dealer catalogs before ordering. Most also send along samples.

Some dealers now offer "chair kits." These are complete packages, including pegs, with enough weaving and binding cane for one chair. These kits are fine if you intend to do only one chair, but if you expect to do several, you'll find it cheaper to buy cane by the full hank.

Preparing to weave

The first step is to clean any old cane from the chair. Even if the old cane seat has disintegrated, you may find remnants in the holes, along with a buildup of dirt, wax, and finishing materials. Sometimes the buildup in the holes turns into fairly solid plugs, and if these can't be cleaned with an awl, use your electric drill with a bit of the correct size to do the job.

If the edges of the chair frame which contact the cane are sharp, use a rasp or coarse file to round them off. This will prevent the edge from cutting the cane. Also, see that the edges of the holes are slightly rounded. If they seem sharp, use a small rat-tail file to ease them a little.

If you intend to refinish the chair as well as to recane it, do all the repair and refinishing work before you begin to weave the cane.

Leave the cane in the hank as it was delivered, and pull each strand from the hank as you need it. Select a strand at the looped end of the hank and pull carefully, shaking the hank as you do to prevent tangling.

Make a coil of the strand with about a 6-in. diameter, with the shiny side of the cane on the outside. Use a spring clothespin or other small clamp to hold the coil.

When handling dry cane, either old or new, be careful to avoid a nasty cut. Some strands have sharp edges which can cut like a razor when dry.

Now immerse the coiled cane (2 or 3 coils at a time) in warm water. Some caners add about 1½ ounces of glycerine per pint of water, but this is optional. Use a wide pan or bowl, and allow the cane to soak about 15 minutes, until it becomes soft and pliable.

Beginning the weaving

Put the chair upright in front of you, so that you look down on the seat from the front as you weave. Begin by counting the holes across the back rail. If there is an odd number of holes, put a peg in the center hole. If there is an even number, put a peg in each of the holes at the center. Do the same at the front rail.

How to order cane

Hole size	Distance between holes	Name of cane size
1/8-in.	3/8-in.	Superfine
3/16-in.	1/2-in.	Fine-fine
3/16-in.	5/8-in.	Fine
1/4-in.	3/4-in.	Narrow medium
1/4-in.	3/4-in.	Medium
5/16-in.	7/8-in.	Common

TO REMOVE THE OLD cane, cut the loops of cane on the bottom with a sharp knife. Be sure you cut every loop completely through.

WHEN ALL LOOPS are cut, you'll be able to lift off the old cane in one piece. Then clean accumulated dirt from the holes with an awl.

PREPARE THE CANE for weaving by coiling it, clamping with a spring clothespin and soaking in warm water for 15 minutes.

PUT CANING PEGS in center holes, then begin at the back and run a strand from back to front. Work from the center to the left.

WEAVE THE CANE back and forth, using pegs to hold it when necessary. Start a new strand whenever necessary.

DON'T WEAVE the cane too tight, since it will tighten later during the weaving process. Allow a little slack to make subsequent steps easier.

AT THE SIDES, cane is not carried all the way to the back holes, but is inserted in side holes. Keep strands parallel.

THE SECOND COURSE is woven across the seat, beginning at the back. The strands lie on top of the first course.

THE THIRD COURSE is woven front to back in the same holes. Put the new cane to the right of the first strand in each hole.

Now take a coil of cane from the water, remove the clamp, and run the cane between your thumb and forefinger to squeegee off any excess water. Put another coil in the water each time you remove one, so that it will be ready when you need it.

As you put in the first course of cane, you work from the center to the left side, then from the center to the right. Remove the peg in the back rail, insert the cane end about 4 inches, and put the peg back in the hole. Now remove the peg at the front, run the entire strand of cane through it, and reinsert the peg.

Move over one hole at the front and bring the strand of cane up through it. Carry the strand to the back rail and down through the second hole. Continue this procedure until all the holes on the left side have been used, then do the same on the right side.

This is the first course of cane. The second

THE FOURTH COURSE is woven across the seat, with the new cane going over Course Three and under Course One strands.

AS YOU COMPLETE the fourth course, the weaving pattern begins to emerge. Work the fourth course from the front to the back.

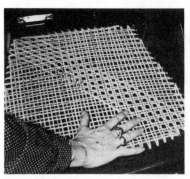

THE FIRST DIAGONAL course begins at the left back. Weave it under the side-to-side strands, over the front-to-back strands.

AS YOU ADD CANE, holes become crowded. Use your awl or an icepick to help make room in each hole for new cane.

LAY THE BINDER cane around the seat edge and secure it by looping regular cane over it at each hole, as shown. This starts the edge trimming.

THE SIZE of the holes in the completed seat depends on the number of holes in the chair rail. The more rail holes, the smaller the cane holes.

course runs across the chair. The procedure is the same, except that you begin at the back and work toward the front. These strands lie on top of the first ones. The third course is from front to back again, using the same holes, but laying each new strand to the right of the first strand in the hole.

The fourth course is woven across the seat, with each new strand going *under* Course One and *over* Course Three. The fifth course is diagonal, from the back left to the front right, with the new strands going *over* the front-to-back strands, and *under* the side-to-side strands. The sixth and last course is diagonal in the opposite direction, woven in the same way. Follow the step-by-step process in the photographs, noting how you tie off cane ends and how you install binder cane.

TO TIE OFF cane ends under the seat, first run the end under the loop which begins in the hole through which the end comes.

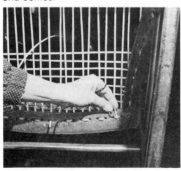

NOW PULL THE END back through the loop formed by its own strand. Keep the cane moist and pliable when tying it off to get a neat, small knot.

FINALLY, pull the tie tight and flat. Making neat tieoffs takes a bit of practice. Trim away excess cane to finish tie.

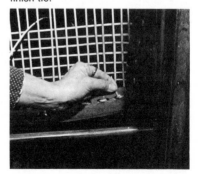

Caning made simple with prewoven rolls

■ TAKE ANOTHER LOOK at that old chair with the hole in its woven seat. See if it has a groove around the edge of the woven portion with a spline in it. If so, machine-woven cane will make the repair easier and less expensive than you might think.

Cane is available in long rolls, 12, 14, 16 and 18 in. wide. A spline is used to wedge it into the seat's groove. Spline comes in diameters of ⅛, 3/16 and ¼ in., with 3/16 in. the most common.

With household shears cut the material roughly to shape, leaving the recommended allowance on all sides. Soak it in warm water (in sink or bathtub) for a half hour or more so the cane will be pliable. Soak the spline for a few minutes, too. Fit it to the groove and cut it ½ in. longer than needed.

Cut about a dozen wedges to hold the cane in the groove. Center the cane on the seat, making sure its glossy side is up and the pattern is not askew. Set the first wedges at front and back; do the same at the sides. Continue this procedure until the caning is taut.

Then use a wedge to force cane into the rest of the groove. Tap lightly with a mallet, being careful not to break the strands.

With a sharp wood chisel, cut off the webbing at the outer edge of the groove and apply glue to the groove. Drive the spline in place using one of the wedges or another small piece of wood.

With a sharp knife, then cut the spline to exact length and drive down the end. The job will look neatest if the ends meet at the center of the seat back.

REMOVE old spline and cane with a wood chisel and clean the groove, being careful not to chip the seat.

A HIGH-SPEED rotary tool is also effective when you're cleaning the old material and glue from groove.

SOAK SPLINE for a few minutes in warm water, fit it to the groove and cut slightly longer than you need.

NEXT, cut the machine-woven cane about 1 in. larger on all sides than the area enclosed by the groove.

STRETCH NEW CANE seat into position using opposing wedges. Use wedge and mallet to tap into groove.

AFTER USING a chisel to cut off the surplus cane, run a generous bead of glue in groove, and drive in spline.

Supercharge your car stereo

■ THERE COMES a day in the life of every car-stereo owner when his basic sound system—usually an AM/FM cassette unit and a pair of speakers—just doesn't excite anymore. It may lack power, or a solid low end, or "shimmer" in the treble or even a few desired control features—but, somehow, the thrill is gone.

On that day, you have two options: Throw out the whole system and start from scratch on a new megabuck setup, or use your existing equipment as you upgrade, adding new components and accessories, one by one.

To illustrate this second approach, we took a well-known sports GT car—a Mercedes-Benz 450SL roadster equiped with a good, basic sound system—and subjected it to a full range of sound-system improvements. The owner of the car had outfitted it with two excellent components which served as our starting points: full-digital AM/FM cassette unit and a pair of 4½-inch full-range speakers, fitted into the small speaker enclosures at the sides of the dash. The sound from this combination was smooth and balanced, with superb radio reception, but it had definite sonic limitations. Here's how we improved it.

We began by extending the frequency range of the system with additional speakers. Most original-equipment car speakers and medium-priced aftermarket units have acceptable response and power-handling capability in the middle ranges; it's in the deep bass and highest treble that their performance is lacking.

To remedy this, we followed the same approach as designers of large home speaker systems: We used specialized speaker drivers that handle the extremes of the music spectrum. At

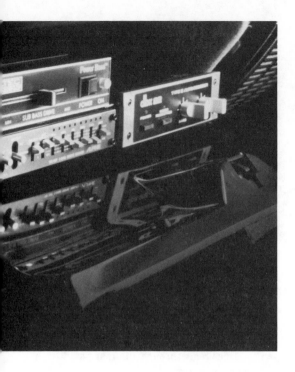

the bass end, we added a subwoofer system which is a 6 × 9 driver with its own built-in amplifier and associated dash-mount control box.

The system is designed to reproduce the range from 20 to 200 Hz, using what engineers call a "long-throw" cone design—a cone capable of moving long distances in and out, thereby moving enough air to pump out high-level bass with minimal distortion. It can be mounted in any mid-size enclosed space: trunk, footwell or even rear side panel, with its control unit up front within easy reach. We dropped one into place behind the seats in the 450SL with about two hours' work. The differences in deep-bass solidity and "oomph" were obvious as soon as we cranked it up.

At the other end of the musical spectrum, a pair of add-on treble units were the key to better high-end definition and a more convincing stereo

CAR SPEAKERS no longer have to be the weak link in your car stereo system. An ultra thin 5-inch coaxial speaker system (above) has been specially designed for car installation. Its depth of only 1⅛-in. makes mounting anywhere in your car easy. Low-frequency response is also possible now with power bass (below) which can provide 107db output at 40w in the 30-150Hz bass range.

POWER AMPLIFIERS (above) can provide output of 50 watts per channel, but are small enough to fit under driver's seat. A 7-band equalizer (below) features a pre-amp fader, optical slide control and LED output level indicator all in the space of a 1-in. high unit.

"image." The idea here was to put the two treble units up as high as possible in the vehicle interior, so that their output blended with and augmented the treble response of the main speakers.

We mounted a pair of tweeters forward in the doors. These speakers consist of 1-inch dome drivers in a sleek, high-tech case with a built-in thumb-wheel level control. In place, their Eurostyle appearance looked just right, and the source of sound had moved upward and acquired a new sharpness—the music now seemed to come from a broad area somewhere on the hood. (All door-mounted speakers, by the way, should be located as far forward as possible to minimize the impact of the slamming doors.)

Another deficiency of the car's original sound system had been a lack of power—the Alpine had only 4 watts per channel built into its chassis. (The manufacturer expected most purchasers to use the cassette deck in conjunction with a separate power amplifier.) The owner of the Mercedes had opted to use it without external amplification. Our interest in setting up the system for wider range sound, though, made a separate power amplifier a necessity.

Power to burn

Though only a single, two-channel power amplifier was needed, we fitted two power amps to illustrate the two basic installation options available. As one approach, we mounted a 50-watt-per-channel amp in the trunk, fastening it to an inner side panel and routing the speaker and power cables back through the rear panel to the passenger compartment.

As an alternative approach—which might be used in a hatchback, a station wagon or a subcompact car—we installed a low-profile, 50-watt-per-channel amplifier under the driver's seat, routing its wiring beneath the floor carpeting to the dash. Both of these locations provide the modest amount of air circulation needed to keep the two amplifiers' operating temperatures within bounds.

Particularly with the convertible top down, the 6 watts per channel from the front-end unit had been adequate for little more than fresh-air background music. The added power from the external amplifiers made it possible to listen at concert-hall volumes and added a sense of unstrained, sonic openness.

In the third phase of our upgrading, we expanded the system's control flexibility—its capacity to be adjusted for proper balance on different types of music. This was accomplished by adding an equalizer to the system, mounting it within the driver's reach in the left-hand side of the glovebox. An equalizer is a sort of expanded tone control. It allows the user to boost or cut the system's tonal response more precisely than conventional bass and treble controls do.

By dividing the musical spectrum into many separate bands, each adjustable with a slider control, an equalizer can be used to balance the deep bass with the mid-bass, the lower mid-range and so on, up through the extreme treble.

The equalizer has five bands per channel, plus illuminated level meters, and an array of secondary controls to be used with rear speakers (which our two-seater project car didn't have).

You can use a car-stereo equalizer two ways: either as a one-time "fix" for your vehicle's acoustical shortcomings, or as a superflexible tone control for the persnickety music listener. In our case, we spent an hour or so adjusting the slider positions, while listening to a variety of musical formats. After that we found that the controls needed little additional fiddling.

We had noticed a lower mid-range hollowness and a bit of mid-treble "sizzle." We were able to rectify both conditions with a few adjustments, further smoothing the sound of what was becoming a first-rate sound system.

Fine-tuning

A couple of additional details rounded out the 450SL's sound equipment. To play back the ultrawide dynamic range, dbx-encoded cassette tapes the car's owner had made on his dbx-equipped home cassette deck, we added an automotive dbx decoder to the array of "black boxes" in the glove compartment. We used it in lieu of the Dolby noise-reduction system built into the unit, but only on cassette encoded in the dbx format.

We also replaced the stock Mercedes antenna—which mounts on the right rear quarter—with an extremely sensitive electronic antenna. It incorporates signal-boosting circuitry built into its cast housing and has a whip length of only 18 inches.

And to connect all of the elements, we used two types of premium low-resistance cables—a heavy-duty, double-jacketed speaker cable and a thick shielded wire for low-level signals. Both are more weather-resistant and freer of stray electrical gremlins like excess capacitance and inductance than conventional wiring. We crimped the speaker connections to spade lugs at each end and covered all wiring splices with heat-shrink tubing.

The final result lived up to our expectations. The upgraded system's sound had an effortless, spacious quality, along with all of the volume and flexibility that an audiophile demands.

THIS COMPLETE AUDIO STEREO SPEAKER SYSTEM includes power bass for low frequencies, midrange speakers, and a hi-frequency pair, all rated at least 40 watts. With this system you will cover the audio frequency range from 5Hz to 18kHz.

Car stereo speaker installation

■ YOU DON'T HAVE to have a pro install your car speakers to get a professional-looking job like the one above. But it pays to do it like the pros do.

First, decide where you want your speakers. Rear-deck speakers are often easiest to install, since many U.S. cars already have the necessary holes. But front mounts—in the doors or front kick panels—give you the best stereo effect in the front seat. And that's the seat most likely to be occupied.

Probably the hardest part of mounting speakers in a door is finding a spot where they won't interfere with structural members or the window mechanism and at the same time won't be placed where the seats will swallow up their sound. Pros know these spots, but you'll have to find them. Loosen the door trim panel, and check out possible speaker sites as you raise and lower the window. Then measure carefully and cut your hole. Use a sabre saw or hacksaw, or drill a circular pattern of holes and saw from one hole to the next. But don't use a power drill or saw on carpet-covered doors—the carpet may tear or run.

To run the speaker wires, remove the inner kick-plate trim (just in front of the door) and drill holes opposite each other in the door edge and door pillar. Line the holes with grommets, so their edges won't cut the insulation. Run wire through the holes to the speakers, and solder them so they can't vibrate loose. Make sure the "hot" leads from each channel of your tape deck go to the same terminal on each speaker, or you'll lose bass response.

For rear-seat speakers, snake the wires unobtrusively through the car by tucking them under the edge of the carpet or floor mats. Where the wires pass the doors, run them under the door saddle (first removing the saddle to clear away gravel or debris that might cut the wires).

To get the wires into the trunk, you must usually remove the rear seat cushion, which is easy. But getting it locked back in again is usually a two-man job. The holes that pass the wire into the trunk should also be grommeted to prevent chafing; it's not a bad idea to caulk the space around the wires, too, against the possibility of exhaust-fume leaks.

Wedge-type, surface-mounting speakers are easiest to mount on the rear shelf, requiring only screw holes for attachment and a grommeted hole for the wire. If the wedge has an open bottom, cutting a larger hole under the speaker will give you better bass response, by letting the trunk act as a resonator.

But wedge speakers can obscure rear vision, and their plastic cases can warp in sunlight. So flush-mount speakers are usually preferred (and many wedges' grilles and speakers can be disassembled and flush-mounted, if you prefer).

Most American cars now have 6x9-inch speaker ovals cut in the metal frame under the rear shelf, often with the deck's fiber covering perforated to form a grille. If your car lacks these perforations, you'll have to cut the fiber. A sharp knife does the cleanest job, but the speaker grille should cover ragged saw-cut edges. If the metal

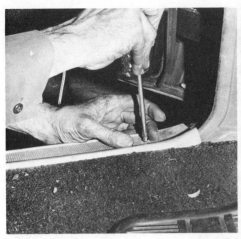

REAR-DECK SPEAKERS ARE EASY TO INSTALL

REAR-DECK SPEAKERS' leads go past the doors most neatly if you unscrew the door saddle (upper left), clear out rough debris that could damage the wires, and run wire under the saddle. Rear-deck mounting is often eased by holes precut for 6×9-in. speakers. If you must cut your own hole, hacksaw work (upper right) can be reduced by drilling a series of holes and sawing between them. Slanting rear windows often prevent the use of a sabre saw from the top of the deck, but you can approach the deck from in the trunk below. Grille cloth can keep small holes from focusing sun on the speaker. Cut it to fit the speaker (lower left) and apply it under the grille (lower right). Avoid plastic grilles on the rear deck; some housings can melt or warp if located there.

is not precut, you'll need a hacksaw or sabre saw. Window overhangs make sabre saws impossible to use from above the shelf on many cars, but if so, you can get in the trunk and cut upward from there. Speaker attachment holes can be poked through the fiber with an icepick; if you have to drill the metal yourself, drill from inside the trunk until the metal is holed, then finish with the icepick. Bolting the speakers in place is easiest if you have a helper in the trunk to hold the speaker nuts and lockwashers as you tighten the screws from above.

Rear-deck speaker grilles should be dark to avoid annoying reflections and preferably not be plastic, which can warp. But metal grilles' small holes (or those in some deck perforations) can

focus the sun's rays like pinhole lenses, sometimes damaging speakers. Here's where an ounce of prevention (or an ounce of grille cloth) is worth lots of cure. Before attaching a metal grille, cover its underside with speaker grille cloth. Cut the cloth to fit the grille and tack it in place with beads of cement around the grille edge.

If you're wiring stereo speakers in both the front and rear of the car, use identical speakers mounted at identical heights for best sound balance. Add-on front-rear stereo balance controls may cause distortion in some installations, but they're cheap, so try them if you like. Four-channel tape decks (and some stereo ones) have built-in connections and balance controls for four speakers.

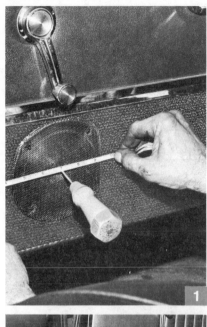
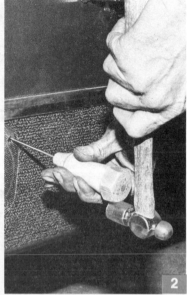

OPEN UP THE DOOR PANEL. IF YOU'VE NEVER DONE IT BEFORE, YOU'LL FIND IT'S EASY TO DO, AND HELPS YOU PINPOINT THE BEST SPEAKER LOCATION

AFTER OPENING THE inside door panel to find the best speaker location, measure the distance on the panel (1); mark, punch and drill mounting holes operating from the most reasonable working position you can find (2); then cut the speaker holes (3). Use care; carpeted door panels are often vulnerable to power tools. Now remove the car's inner kick-plate panel (4); drill the panel and door edge; and thread the wire (4 and 5). Grommets are a smart idea. Run leads to the speaker (6) and solder them, positive to the same post on each speaker. Position the speaker, align the holes (7), and mount the speaker and grille (8). Use self-tapping screws if the door is metal, speed nuts or washers and lockwashers if it's fiber. The grille shown here matches the car's interior, but a chrome grille, is significantly more scuff-resistant.

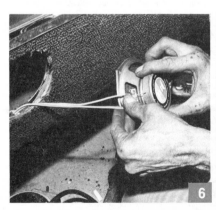

Carpentry: an introduction

■ CARPENTRY IS THE craft of using wood in the construction or finishing of buildings or similar structures. Carpentry extends from building the forms for a foundation to finishing off window frames in the interior rooms. Between these points, *rough carpentry* includes putting up wall studs, installing floor and ceiling joists, rafter layout and placing and nailing shingles on the roof. *Finish carpentry* includes cutting and installing finish moldings and paneling for walls, putting in windows and doors and laying floors.

A carpenter must have many skills. You can start from below ground as a carpenter and not be done until the last ridge piece is nailed in place. Then there's the opportunity for carpentry skills in filling a house with shelves, cabinets and furniture.

Almost anyone willing to learn these skills can. Basic to all carpentry skills is the fact that the more patience applied to any piece of work, the more likely the job is to go quickly and correctly the first time.

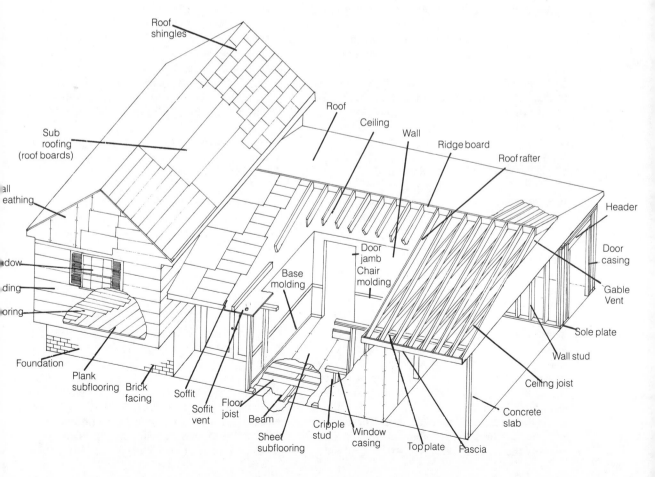

Rough carpentry

Rough carpentry starts with foundations. These can be simple poles or piers buried below the frost line or they can be complex full basements, crawl spaces or pads. While most of the work in foundations more properly involves masonry skills, it is at the sills that the skills of carpentry are essential.

Sills. For standard construction, sill plates are normally made of 2 × 6 lumber. Special needs may require larger or smaller sills. The sill plates must be anchored properly to the foundations. Sills are made either of pressure-treated wood or are protected with a metal termite shield that extends at least 1 in. on each side of the sill plate, then bends downward at about a 30° angle for another inch. Sills are anchored with ½-in.-dia. bolts set into the concrete or wood of the foundation before the sills are laid. Sills must be placed so no joints occur over openings in the foundation. They are butt-jointed.

Beams and girders. Beams and girders are the structural members used to support the structure and distribute the loads between supports. The terms *beam* and *girder* are interchangeable, though on occasion wood members are called beams and steel members are called girders. Floor joists will run off the beams to support the floors.

Beam size is carefully chosen to support the intended load with the minimum allowable deflection of the beam. In many small buildings, no beam is needed because the joists themselves will be strong enough to provide proper support over the specified span (the distance between two supporting columns or foundation walls).

Joists. The strength specifics vary with the type of wood used as joists. Southern pine is among the strongest and hemlock among the weakest of commonly used woods. For 24-in. on-center spacing of joists, and a 40-lb.-per-square-foot live load, a 2 × 8 pine joist can span 11 ft. 5 in. If your structure is wider (17 ft. 9 in., for example), you should go for 2 × 12 joists. If you space your joists on 16-in. centers, a 2 × 8 pine joist can span 13 ft. 1 in. and a 2 × 12 would be best for a span of about 20 ft. 4 in. For greater widths, you'll need a beam. Local building codes may specify different lengths for spans and loads of a particular wood, so it is always best to check the codes before completing your plans and ordering your lumber.

Subfloors. Because today's construction is almost all platform style, subfloors go down as soon as the joists are in place. Almost all subflooring is now done with plywood in appropriate grades and thicknesses for the on-center distances of the joists. Conventionally, a subfloor of ½-in. CD plywood is considered sufficient for 16-in. on-center work. If the plywood is laid over a 2-ft. on-center distance, it is best to go with ⅝-in. plywood.

Install the subfloor with 6d common nails at 6-in. intervals on the panel edges and 10-in. intervals on the interior. Nail spacing may be wider if a construction adhesive is used (nail at 1-ft. intervals). If you are using ⅝-in. plywood, use 8d nails. Common nails are a minimum choice, and ring or other deformed-shank nails give stronger results.

If you use board subflooring, you face more work. Use nominal 1-in. sheathing lumber no more than 6 in. wide, and the subflooring crosses the joists at a 45° angle. Use two 8d nails at each joist. Board subflooring, which has been used for decades, is quite strong but is more labor-intensive because of the angle cuts. The nailing pattern is spread out because each board length must be nailed at each joist as it is installed. These lengths can reach 16 ft.

Wall framing. Wall framing in almost all construction today is done on 16-in. or 24-in. centers. Because 24-in. on-center is often considerably cheaper and faster to put up, it is used more as codes are changed to reflect the economies and other advantages. There are stricter standards for sheathing and siding thickness than for 16-in. on-center work.

A sole plate is laid on the subfloor and the wall framed to the sole plate. Sole plates and studs are the same size material.

Today, most walls are framed in sections while they're lying on the subfloor. The walls are then tipped into place, plumbed and braced. Once the wall is up, the sole plate is nailed through the subfloor. Walls can also be framed one piece at a time, but more work is required and nailing is more difficult.

Wall studs are usually 2 × 4s placed on 16-in. centers. When wall stud spacing moves out to 24-in. on-center, the wider spacing may require 2 × 6 wall studs. On outside walls this is an advantage, since thicker insulation can be installed. Usually, 2 × 6 studding on 24-in. centers will be about equal in cost to 2 × 4 studding on 16-in. centers, once both material and labor have been figured (the larger studs use one-third fewer members, reducing the labor by a fair amount).

Studs are capped with double top plates, fastened one row at a time with 16d nails. If the wall is to be tilted into place, the nailing job is quite simple. Corners require some special spacing of both studs and top plates. One top plate overlaps the one underneath to provide extra strength. Corners need to be built with an extra stud to provide a nailer for interior walls.

Windows and doors. Window and door installation is critical to good carpentry. If it is not plumb and level, even the most expensive and sturdy will not open or close right. Both windows and doors have headers of 2 × 6 or 2 × 8 material, with spacers used to bring them out to the wall framing thickness. Trimmer studs, set inside a full stud, support the headers. The trimmer studs are nailed to the full studs to provide more strength than the standard nail.

The bottoms of windows rest on a sill of the same material as the rest of the framing. The sill is supported by short jack, or cripple, studs. Very short studding is often required above doors and windows to bring the top plate in contact with the top of the headers.

In most construction, the level of the top of doors and windows are installed at the same height to give a neat line and make installation of sheathing and siding simpler. These openings, like all framing carpentry, are classed as rough. Usually there is an overall allowance of an inch or two above the size of the assembled window or door unit so that shim stock can bring the unit to its final plumb and level.

Roof framing. The most difficult part of carpentry to plan and start is the roof framing. Even a simple gable end roof requires the use of the rafter framing square, a tool with which many home workers are not familiar. With experience, such framing can easily be done from scales provided right on the square. Whether you use the

THE SUPPORT for all carpentry work in a house is the foundation walls and either wood beams or metal girders (shown here). Other wood structures are built on the concrete slabs, anchored by bolts set in the concrete as shown in the future garage area here.

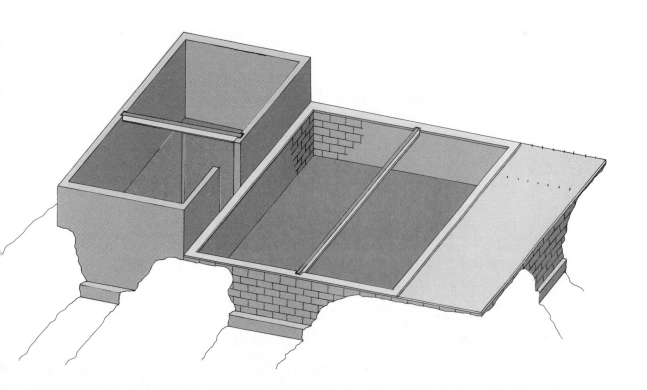

framing square or the "step-off" method, the job begins with ceiling joists.

Ceiling joists. Ceiling joists provide a nailing surface for ceiling materials and tie the walls together. Ceiling joists are usually placed next to the spots where rafters will be installed. When trusses are used, joists are not needed.

Spans up to about 16½ ft. need 2 × 8 joists on 24-in. centers. The use of 16-in. centers lets 2 × 8 joists span as much as 19 ft. For spans to 22 ft. with 24-in. centers, or 24 ft. with 16-in. centers, use 2 × 10s. These sizes are meant to support no more than a 20-lb.-per-square-foot live load. Check your local building codes for requirements in your area. If the codes say you must build to support a greater load, then heavier joists may be needed.

Ceiling joists are usually placed next to the spots where the rafters will be installed.

Rafters. Rafters are also selected for particular spans and loadings. The span must also vary, depending on wind and snow loadings in your area, as well as on roof slope. Your local codes or a building supply house should provide you with rafter size requirements for your area.

The rafter used in a gabled roof is called a common rafter. You need one pattern rafter per roof if the sides of the roof are of equal length and slope. Start your pattern rafter with a good straight piece of material. Remember, all length requirements are taken on the center line of the rafter unless the plans say otherwise. The framing square can be used to find the length of the

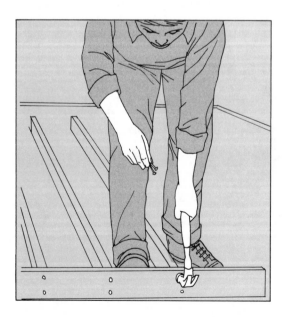

stock needed for the rafters. After you make the cuts on your pattern rafter, check its fit. Bring the ridge line to plumb and check the height of the rise. It's best to check right at the top plate because you can check the fit of the bird's mouth, if any, as well as the rise and the fit of the ridge board. If everything fits, use the rafter as a pattern to mark and cut the others. Check each rafter as it is cut.

Wall sheathing. You have a choice of placing wall sheathing before or after framing the roof. The rafters or trusses provide extra strength, however, helping to keep framed walls from bowing out of plumb. With subfloor materials already in place, it is usually better to get the roof on before closing in the walls to protect against the weather.

Wall sheathing always starts at a corner of the framing. With today's method of letting the sheathing replace other forms of bracing, it's best to do all corners before moving in on the walls. Even when sheathing and siding is combined in a single material, the start is at the corners. As much of a full panel of plywood as possible is securely nailed with galvanized nails spaced 6 in. along the outside edges and 8 in. along the interior. The plywood sheathing is installed vertically, and under most codes today is all that is required as bracing.

With all sheathing, subflooring and other similar materials, joints have to fall over studs or joists. If plywood sheathing is installed with the long edge horizontal, nailers have to be added at the top edge.

Finish carpentry

Once any structure is framed, subfloored and sheathed, the next step is *finish carpentry*. Rough carpentry has taken care of the work until now, but finish work involves installation of windows, doors, stairs and ornamental work such as moldings, casings, baseboards and other trim. Roofing is also classed as finish carpentry, but like siding using modern materials, roofing is fairly simply done with modern asphalt and asphalt-fiberglass shingle materials.

Soffits and fascia. Exterior finish work consists mostly of installing soffits and fascia boards at the eave overhangs. It also includes building or enclosing that area, known as the *cornice*. A cornice may be open or closed (boxed). Open cornices allow the rafter ends to show. They will usually have a section of molding set between the rafters, at the house wall line, to prevent air infiltration. Closed cornices are more complex. Lookouts are added to form right angles with the wall lines. The lookouts then have a soffit nailed to them, with ventilation screening in place to allow air movement between the rafters but to keep insects and animals out. A fascia, or face, board is added to the rafter ends as a finish piece. If the fascia overhangs the soffit edge, a section of molding is used there to give the unit a completed appearance.

Doors and windows. Interior finish work includes installing windows and doors. Today almost all windows and doors are installed in packages known as prehung units.

Once the rough opening is framed, the door or window is placed on its sill, centered and shimmed to both plumb and level. The units must be plumb in both directions; the plumb must be from side to side as well as from front to back of the window or door casing. Shim stock, usually cedar shingles, is used to be sure the units are plumbed and level and stay that way.

Window units are tacked in place at the bottom corners of the mounting flange or exterior trim. Nails or screws are driven through the finish sill and shims into the rough frame. Window units are normally fastened with 6-in. 6d galvanized common nails about 8 in. apart.

Door units are fastened to the rough door framing by driving 8d finishing nails through the jambs and shims. Use 1d finishing nails to attach the casing to the rough door framing near the outside edge. Space nails every 16 in. Use 8d galvanized finishing or casing nails every 16 in. through the jambs to complete the job. To finish, casing should be added to the back side of the prehung door unit and the stop molding nailed into the jambs.

Flooring. Flooring is a part of finish carpentry. Wood flooring is usually finished off with a baseboard molding made in two or three pieces. The baseboard goes in place against the floor and wall, with a shoe molding against the baseboard and floor. The shoe molding is quarter round, big enough so that any remaining gaps are closed. It is nailed to the flooring with finishing nails.

FLOOR JOISTS rest on the foundation and girder. These support the subfloor, which can be either individual boards (shown here) or sheets of plywood or other material. The walls are erected on sill plates anchored to the floor or to the concrete foundation.

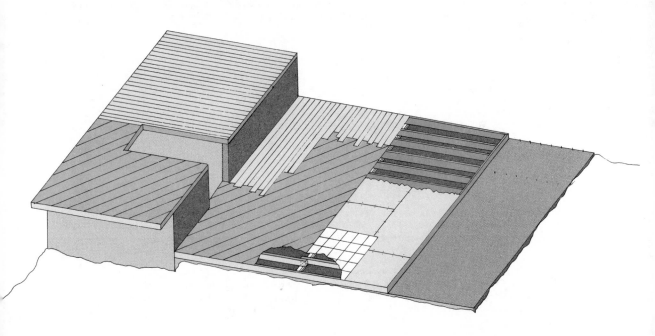

INSTALLING DOOR CASINGS

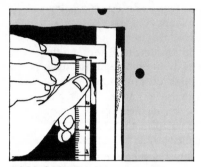

DOOR CASING (trim) should be set back a uniform distance from jamb edge; ¼ in. is the usual reveal. Mark setback in several places.

CUT MITER at one end of casing, then mark casing length from inside corner. The length of the casing includes the ¼-in. reveal.

TO INSTALL DOOR (and window) casings, use 4d finishing nails through thin edge into jamb, and 6d nails through thick edge into stud about 10 to 12 in. apart.

TO GUARANTEE that miter joints will stay closed, cut header casing to suit span between vertical casings. Then apply glue sparingly to mating surfaces.

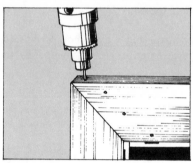

NEXT, BORE slightly undersize lead holes through joint. The bit you select should provide a tight fit for the finishing nail that follows.

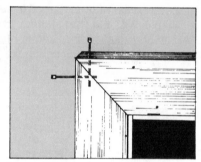

SECURE JOINT with two 6d finishing nails. Set the nails with nailset.

BASE MOLDING TIPS

CORRECT door-trim detail at floor. Door casing extends to floor and baseboard trim abuts the casing.

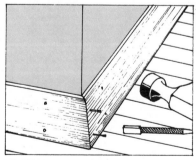

TO KEEP an outside corner miter closed, first apply glue to miter. Then secure it with 4d finishing nails.

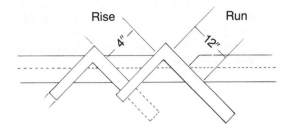

Rise Run

4" 12"

A FRAMING square can be used to find the length of the stock needed for the rafters. Because of the angle of the rise from the wall to the ridge, the beam will be longer than the flat distance between the edge and the center of the span. Use the framing square to get an approximate length of the rafter material. Set the rise on the tongue (shorter, narrower part) of the square; the run on the longer part. A 4-ft. rise converts to 4 in. on the square, a 12-ft. run converts to 12 in. Step off these marks 12 times down the length of the board (for a 12-ft. run) and you'll get the rough length of the board you need. Be sure to allow for overhang.

There may also be a cap molding placed on top of the plain baseboard.

Resilient, ceramic and other flooring types have their own special moldings and finish methods.

Interior trim. Once the floor is in and the drywall is up, taped, primed and painted, the rest of the interior trim is installed. Casings around doors and windows are added, if they are not part

of the prehung units. Crown molding at the joint of the ceiling and wall is still used today, and may require a bit of fancy cutting. New tools, such as the compound miter, make the job easier, but a plain coping saw can produce a coped joint that is quite attractive.

All finish work is done with finishing or casing nails, using a nail set with the finishing nails. Fill the holes with a wood putty.

WALL STUDS are placed 16 or 24 in. apart on-center. They are nailed to a single sole plate on the bottom and a double 2 × 4 top plate. Openings for doors and windows require headers to support the weight over the opening.

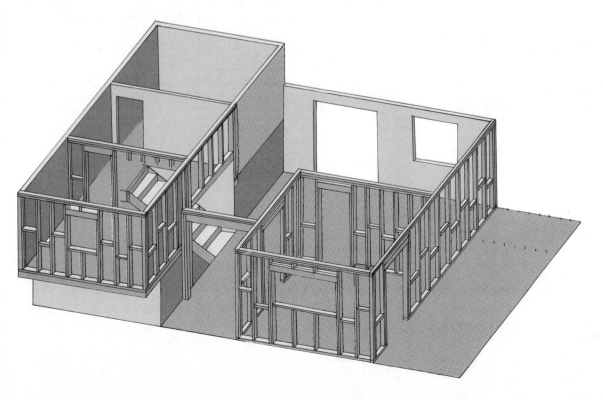

Pro's tips on finish carpentry. The finish carpentry that you are most likely to encounter as a homeowner will involve "trimming out" a room. This includes installation of those moldings and trim intended to conceal joints and framing details and give the room a finished appearance. Such carpentry work also includes the application of baseboards, door and window casings, outside corner guards, ceiling moldings, chair rails and the like.

TIPS ON FINISH CARPENTRY

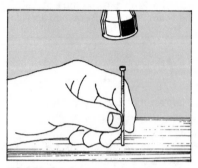

TO DRIVE A finishing nail, grasp it between the thumb and index finger and start nail with several light taps.

NEVER DRIVE a finishing nail home with a hammer. Instead, stop when nail is about ⅛ in. above the surface.

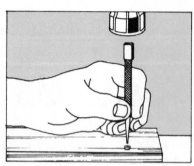

POSITION NAILSET in head's dimple and set with one or two sharp raps. hold nailset so it won't damage wood.

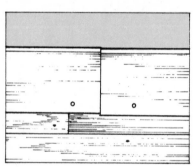

WRONG WAY to install long run of baseboard: with square-cut ends simply abutted.

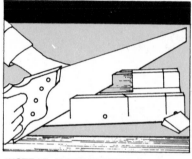

INSTEAD, MAKE JOINTS in long runs using a miter. Use miter box for accuracy.

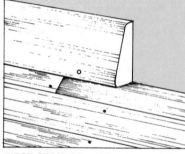

FIRST STRIP OF molding has an open miter. Nail it in place before installing next strip.

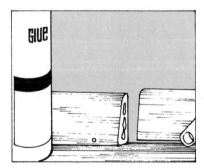

APPLY GLUE to the miter surfaces, then install the second piece of molding.

SECURE MITER joint with 3d (1¼-in.) nails through the joint.

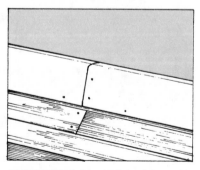

CLOSE THE finished joint tightly, and it will stay that way.

ROOFING WITH modern materials is a relatively simple job, though the hazards of working in high places must be kept in mind and safety practices must be followed.

CEILING JOISTS are nailed to the double top plates. After the roof rafters are in place, roof boards are installed to provide support for the roofing material and shingles. Prehung windows and doors are installed in the wall openings and other trim finish construction.

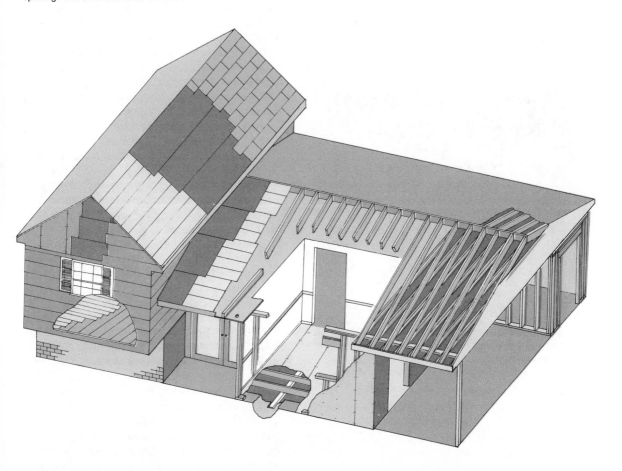

THE CIRCULAR saw is the most popular tool used in rough carpentry. A 7¼-in. model provides the cutting power and depth needed for almost all jobs; carbide blades stay sharper longer.

A SABRE saw is helpful for notching beams, cutting curves and special designs. It can also be used on straight cuts when used with a straightedge guide and a lot of practice.

Tools for carpentry

The carpenter's tool box contains basic equipment for measuring, cutting and fastening.

Handsaws. Three basic kinds of handsaws are used in carpentry work: The crosscut and ripsaw are more commonly used in rough carpentry work, and the backsaw is useful for finish carpentry.

The teeth on a crosscut saw are wider than the blade. This prevents the blade from clogging and binding in the kerf. A good crosscut saw for general rough carpentry use will have 10 teeth to the inch and a blade length of about 26 in. Eight-point saws (bigger teeth) cut more quickly, but the cuts are rougher.

Ripsaws have fewer teeth per inch, and these are set parallel with the blade like a series of chisels along the edge.

Backsaws are used when cutting exact angles in trim and moldings. The blade is rectangular instead of tapered like the crosscut or ripsaw. Because the backsaw is used for more exact cutting, there are up to 16 teeth per inch for a finer cut line. A miter box is usually used with a backsaw. Grooves in the miter box guide the backsaw blade into exact angles to the board.

Power saws. The power saw is the most common tool, and for general work both the panel handsaw and the circular saw are popular.

The circular saw will do almost everything the panel saw will do, and do it far more quickly. But it can't cut into corners and stop with accuracy, so both saws are needed.

Sabre saws. Sabre saws are also handy in both rough and finish carpentry. These saws are variously known as jigsaws and scroll saws, depending on their exact design. Use them for notching beams, cutting curves and making specially designed pieces.

Routers. Routers are often overlooked tools for making interior cuts. They are also used for trimming edges and for making specially designed edges.

Chisels. Chisels come in several forms and a variety of names. Beveled edge chisels are meant for relatively light, accurate wood removal. Mortising chisels have no beveled edges and are meant for hollowing out thick sections of wood to accept tenons in mortise-and-tenon joints. These two are the ones you're most likely to need.

Hammers. Rough carpentry usually requires a 16-oz. claw hammer. For finish work, many professional carpenters prefer to use the lighter 13-oz. hammer. But if you are doing trim work that requires hefty finishing nails (10d or heavier), you should switch back to your 16-ouncer, especially when you're using the nailset.

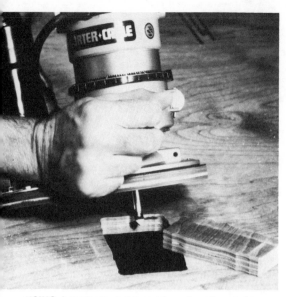

USING A router to make an internal cut is not always considered, but certain bits are exceptionally useful for the purpose, especially on plywood. It can also be used to trim edges.

GOOD SUPPORT is a primary need for all woodworking and carpentry. Sawhorses such as these save building your own and are sturdier than most jobs require. To keep from cutting the tops of your sawhorses, all work can be supported on two or more scrap 2 × 4s, as shown.

A COMPOUND miter saw cuts materials up to 2 × 4s accurately. It is easy to adjust the precise cuts for use in moldings and interior trim.

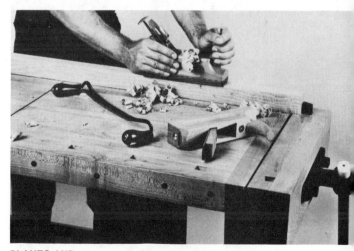

PLANES AND other woodworking tools have many uses in carpentry. Tools shown here include a reform plane (being used), a scrub plane (for use on rough lumber) and a draw knife. The reform plane is for final shaping and smoothing.

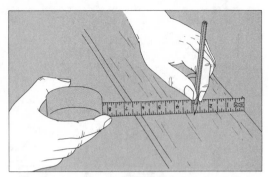

THE EDGE of the measuring tape is tipped so the markings are placed directly on the piece to be marked, eliminating any error in reading measurements.

Measuring

There is an old saying that measuring twice means cutting once. Accurate measurements are the mark of a good craft worker in any field, and the proper use of measuring tools is the primary way to get accurate measurements.

Most long measurements are made with a retractable steel measuring tape. Use folding rules or straightedges for the shorter distances. When using a measuring tape, folding rule or straight rule, always tip the blade so the marking is close to the work surface. All metal measuring tapes

curve up at the edges, often giving a gap of ⅜ in. between work surfaces and measuring marks. Reduce that gap and you reduce the chance of error. Wood and metal rules have different thicknesses, but the same technique is used on both: hold the rule on edge, so the measurements are directly against the work surface, then make your mark.

When measuring a long piece, use a helper to make sure the starting end of the rule or tape is held in its correct spot. You can also use a tool with a hook on it so it holds itself in place.

A chalk line can be used to mark long cuts. When using a chalk line, have your helper hold one end in place, align the line carefully, then lift the line straight up from its path and release it to snap your mark. Whenever possible, use a straightedge and carpenter's pencil or metal-tipped scribe to make marks instead of a chalk line. The mark is thinner and far more accurate.

There are three kinds of squares usually found in a carpenter's toolbox. Squares are used to mark for crosscuts and to help align parts at right angles to each other. The try square has a rigid 6- or 12-in. arm connected to a handle to form an "L". For larger jobs, the framing square also has tables on either side to help make measurements for wall braces, rafters or stairs. The combination square, with its sliding blade, can also mark 45° angles and can help you mark long rip

THE SLIDING T is a tool for layout other than 45° and 90° angles. Note how the point of the pen used to make the mark is pointed into the edge by the board.

THE SQUARE and scribe make a fine combination. The scribe makes a thin, accurate mark on the 90° or 45° angle measured by the square.

cuts. This is one tool where cost should not be the primary factor in your selection. Cheap squares go out of square the first or second time they're handled roughly—or dropped on the job.

A final necessary measuring tool is the bubble level. These come in many sizes and shapes. For general use, one 2 ft. long is best. It can be aluminum, magnesium or mahogany. The level contains bubbles to indicate accuracy both level (horizontal) and plumb (vertical). Little skill is required to use the level: When the bubbles are within the marks on their tubes, the material is accurately placed.

Do-it-yourself carpentry projects

There are many projects in which you can develop or polish your carpentry skills in this 27-volume set of *Popular Mechanics Do-It-Yourself Encyclopedia.*

You can increase your knowledge and skills in using **hand tools** from the material in Volume 12. All kinds of **power tools** are introduced in Volume 19, with specific treatment of **circular saw** techniques in Volume 6, the **bench saw** in Volume 3, and **sabre saws** and techniques for using the **radial-arm saw** in Volume 20. A complete guide to your use of nails, screws and other types of **fasteners** is part of Volume 9.

Additional information on the all-important aspect of **measurements** is treated in Volume 16, with special emphasis on measuring and cutting **angles** in Volume 1. A better understanding of lumber and wood is yours in the part of Volume 26 that deals with **woods and woodworking.**

Most of the homeowner's carpentry skills will be put to use in remodeling; you'll find some general **remodeling** projects in Volume 20, specific projects for **basement remodeling** in Volume 2 and for **home improvement** projects in Volume 13.

You can find ideas for rough carpentry in the projects about **home additions** in Volume 13 and for **garages** in Volume 11. You can cap off your rough carpentry with the projects about **roofs** in Volume 19 and **siding** in Volume 22.

Help with projects about finish carpentry include **doors** (Volume 7) and **windows** (Volume 26). A complete treatment of **floors and flooring** in Volume 10 will give you help with this aspect of carpentry. If you want to try your hand at **paneling,** you should consult Volume 17. Polish your finish carpentry skills with the projects and specific directions for **joinery** in Volume 14 and add the finishing touch of **moldings** in Volume 16.

Other projects for your carpentry skills can be found in the treatment of **porches** in Volume 19 and **stairs** in Volume 22. Many smaller construction projects are in the material about **yard and garden shelters** in Volume 27.

Surface boards the expert way

■ WHEN A WOODWORKING project like a table, desk or cabinet calls for wide, solid-lumber panels, your chance of getting single boards to do the job is almost impossible. And even if you could find them, the chance the boards are flat is just as slim. Uusally, you have to edge-join a number of boards to get the required widths.

Ideally, you should be able to glue up the proper number of flat and true boards, then merely finish-sand the piece to complete it. But in reality it doesn't work that way. The boards are bound to have defects that are compounded once they are joined.

Such faults as cup (a crosswise warp), bow (a lengthwise warp) and twist (a diagonal warp) will be present to one degree or another. Sometimes a combination of these faults occurs in a single board. The stock may also come in varying thicknesses, not only between different boards but also within a single board. All will require surfacing to obtain smooth and flat stock.

Surfacing options

Depending on the amount of material that has to be removed and the equipment you have in your shop, surfacing can be done with hand tools, portable power tools and stationary shop equipment. A cabinet scraper, jack plane and jointer plane are all good tools for light surfacing, especially when they are properly sharpened. A belt sander—followed by an orbital finishing sander—is also a good surfacing choice when removal requirements are thin.

But if a board or assembly is especially warped, heavier-duty equipment makes more sense. A router and a circular saw, when used with easy-to-build jigs, can make short work of flattening any large panel, as can a rotary planer attachment in a radial-arm saw. A jointer and thickness planer can mill boards smooth and flat before assembly, which drastically reduces the surfacing time once the panel is glued up.

Preparation

Regardless of the surfacing method you choose, there are certain things you can do before assembly to minimize distortion. First, you should arrange your component boards so the flattest possible surface is obtained before assembly. If boards are bowed, make it a policy to butt the edges with opposing curves together so the inherent stresses in one board will tend to neutralize those in the other and keep the assembly flat.

Also, if boards are cupped, you can avoid cumulative warp by inverting alternate boards so an end view of the grouping will show a shallow up-and-down wave pattern instead of one deep curve. Another way to effectively reduce warp is to rip the defective board or boards into narrower pieces and then edge-join these smaller boards into a larger slab. While this may seem like extra work, the time required is significantly less than surfacing a severely distorted panel, especially if you are using hand tools.

Finish surfacing

Once you have your stock flat and relatively smooth, finish-sanding is required when using any method except the cabinet scraper. This is best done with a progression from coarse (80-grit) through fine (180- to 220-grit) sandpaper. Each grit should remove scratches from the previous abrasive until no scratches are noticeable to the touch or eye.

Three simple ways to join boards

There are several ways to edge-join boards to make up wider assemblies. If the finished slab will be subject to stresses, such as a workbench or kitchen countertop, a dowel-reinforced joint is the best choice. But when the joint line won't be stressed as much, the nail/pin method can be

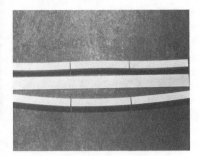

ALTERNATE THE cup direction of the boards before assembly (top), or the finished panel will have a deep cup warp (bottom) once it is joined. The straight board in the middle is shown for reference.

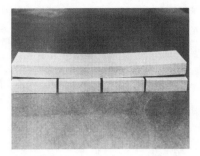

A CUPPED board also can be partially straightened before assembly by ripping it into narrower boards, which will lie flatter. The boards shown were cut from the same piece of stock.

BEFORE USING any method to flatten old surfaces, remove or sink imbedded nails and other impediments that could damage tools.

1 To join stock with dowels, bore ¾-in.-deep holes every 12 in. in both boards. Use dowel centers for accuracy. Insert a 1¼-in.-long dowel in each hole.

2 Make pins from 4d finishing nails by cutting off heads. Bore pilot holes in one board and insert blunt end of pins. Glue board edges and clamp together.

3 Edge-gluing is all that's needed to join straight flat boards. Use a thin layer of aliphatic glue on edges; let it set for 5 minutes and clamp boards together.

ONE CLEVER way to find high spots on a wide panel before hand surfacing is to rub a straight stick—with carbon paper taped to its bottom edge—over the workpiece.

ANOTHER WAY to find high spots is to wedge a pencil into a hole in a small block, then slide the block across a straight board at 2-in. intervals along the panel's surface.

used. These serve to keep the slightly warped boards aligned during clamping. They do not add much strength to the joint. If your stock is flat and smooth before assembly, aliphatic resin glue is all that's needed. It becomes tacky when exposed to air for five minutes and provides enough grab to keep boards from sliding out of alignment when clamped. To make all edges straight and square before assembly, use a power jointer or hand jointer plane.

Cabinet scraper

This tool makes a very fine cut and is ideal when the stock requires only minimal surfacing, such as flattening wood fibers along a joint line. It also works well for removing previous tool marks such as planer ripples. For wide panels, it is best used in a tool handle. When properly sharpened, it produces extremely thin shavings. The tool can be used across the grain, but the finish passes should always be made with the grain.

WHEN A cabinet scraper cuts powdery shavings like those shown, it's time to resharpen. To do so, pull a burnisher over each edge 4 to 5 times at a 10° to 15° angle.

Jack plane

A jack plane can remove stock quickly, and with practice it's simple to control. But it does have two basic requirements: The plane iron must be very sharp, and the tool should never be worked against the grain.

First, find the high spots on the slab by using either a metal straightedge or the carbon paper trick shown. Then make the initial cuts diagonally to remove the highest spots. Finish up by making continuous full strokes from one end to the other with the blade adjusted for a fine cut.

WHEN USING a bench planer to surface a wide panel, begin by making diagonal strokes to chop down high spots. Finish with strokes that match the direction of the wood grain.

Jointer plane

Jointer planes, sometimes called trying planes, are the ancestor of today's power shop jointer. They are available in steel or wood models and come in a variety of lengths: 20, 22 and 24 in. for steel planes and up to 26 in. long for some wood planes.

Their extreme sole length allows them to smooth stock easily without following the minor ups and downs in the surface, the way shorter planes do. Because of this, they are effective for surfacing both individual boards and rough sub-assemblies—like the ones shown—before they are joined into wider assemblies.

They are usually used in basically the same way as jack planes, but their length does limit their usefulness to longer stock.

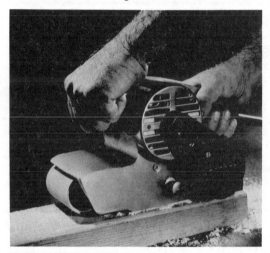

WHEN BELT-SANDING at the end of a panel, apply greater downward pressure at the rear of the tool and lift the front slightly to prevent rounding over the edge.

Belt sander

The belt sander is better for surfacing wide assemblies than narrow individual boards and is the tool of choice when the grain direction alternates from end to end within a panel or one of the component boards. It works by abrasion instead of cutting so there is no risk of chipping the surface. The tool, however, is very powerful and can dig deep depressions into stock if it is not kept moving continually. Even a slight hesitation in one spot can cause damage.

For initial surfacing on rough assemblies, the tool does require some finesse. Use an 80-grit belt and hold it firmly in both hands. Apply more downward pressure when the sander is in contact with the high spots, and release the pressure so it will glide over the low spots. Once the panel is basically flat, install a 120-grit belt and apply equal pressure across the entire surface.

Be careful when you reach the ends of a panel because this tool will quickly grind away the edge. When you are done, switch to a finishing sander and work through a progression of coarse to fine grits (120 to 220) until the surface is free of all scratches.

Power plane

For rough surfacing, a power plane performs well. It does not, however, yield a ready-to-sand surface because the cutters are narrow and the tool base is relatively short. It must be followed with a hand plane or belt sander for best results.

After making diagonal cuts to knock over the high spots, direct the tool in the direction of the grain. Begin at one edge and make continuous passes from end to end, barely lapping each cut.

A POWER PLANE removes stock quickly but can be difficult to control. Keep the depth-of-cut shallow and begin working diagonally. Then plane lengthwise in grain direction.

Jointer

A 4-in. jointer used to joint board edges also can be a valuable surfacing aid. Although its capacity is small, many projects like cabinet door rails and stiles and table aprons are frequently no wider than 4 in.

To use the machine, just slide the board along the bed and over the cutters taking off 1/16-in.— or less—stock each pass until the board is flat. Be sure to cut with the grain, and always use a rubber faced push block in your rear hand to keep your fingers away from the moving cutters.

Planer

Remember that a thickness planer is designed to smooth boards, but not necessarily to flatten them. This is because the feed rollers that draw the stock into the cutters tend to flatten out any warped board before it's cut. A uniform shaving is taken off the entire surface, not just the high spots. When the board emerges from the other side, it will revert back to its original shape, the warp still intact.

A good way to avoid the problem is shown below. When the tool is used this way, it will smooth and flatten stock at the same time. And it can be used for individual boards or subassemblies that are to be joined into wider panels later.

Router

To use your router as a surfacing tool, you must first build the jig shown. This can be made from scrap wood, but all parts must be straight and flat. The width of the jig between the top cleats should match the width of your router base, and the distance between the lower jig boards should be just slightly wider than the workpiece.

Once the jig is built, nail a support strip to both sides of the workpiece, letting each extend about 6 in. beyond both ends. Position these strips so their top edges align perfectly.

With a 3/4-in.-dia. carbide-tipped straight cutter in the router, begin cutting. When each pass is complete, slide the jig over 5/8 in. and make another cut until the whole surface is smooth and flat. Finish up with a hand plane or belt sander.

Circular saw

The key to surfacing all stock is to set up a milling arrangement that will cut to the same depth relative to a true horizontal plane, not to the surface that is being milled. In the router method, this was accomplished with a wood jig

HARDWOODS, such as maple, are not flattened by feed rollers. Push board through with convex side of cup pointing up, then turn board over and push through again.

SOFTWOOD STOCK, like pine, will be flattened by rollers. To avoid this, nail shim into cup hollow, even with board edges. Use short brads that clear path of cutters.

RUN BOARD through planer with shim in place. Shim prevents rollers from flattening board so proper stock is removed. Then turn the board over and plane the other side.

SAW KERF-CUTTING is a good choice for surfacing wide soft wood assemblies like fir bench top. First step is to mark both ends square to find the approximate cut depth.

SHAVE WASTE to bottom of saw kerfs using hand plane across grain. Then plane with grain to remove tool marks. Surface will be smooth, flat and straight.

INSTALL LEVEL guide strips on each side of top and build jig similar to one shown for router. Start saw and push through jig, making all successive cuts about ½ in. apart.

that moved along two guide strips on the sides of the slab. The same technique is used to turn a circular saw into a surfacing tool. The jig is built the same way, but with the dimensions altered so the top cleats are spaced to match the width of the circular saw's shoe.

Nail the guide strips to the slab so their top edges are parallel and the strips extend 6 in. beyond both ends of the workpiece. Place the jig on the strips and slide it up and down the slab to determine what the low point of the surface is relative to the jig. Set the saw blade depth to just graze this low point. Then start kerf-cutting the surface. Move the jig about ½ in. between cuts. When the surface is all cut, remove the jig and plane across the grain to chip off the waste. Plane with the grain for final surfacing.

Radial-arm saw

To use your radial-arm saw as a surfacing machine requires a rotary planer attachment. Its cutting head has three carbide-tipped blades and is attached directly to the saw arbor. It can surface widths twice the length of the saw arm and lengths equal to one-half the length of the saw table. To surface longer panels, add temporary extension tables to the sides of your saw table.

Add support strips and adjust the cutter height so the blades will graze the lowest part of the slab. Position the cutter at the rip fence and lock in place. Then feed the work under the cutter from left to right, advancing the yoke outward after each pass until the slab is completely surfaced. The tool does leave marks that will have to be removed with a plane or belt sander later.

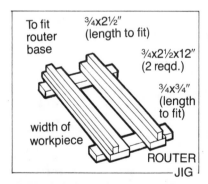

To fit router base

¾x2½" (length to fit)

¾x2½x12" (2 reqd.)

¾x¾" (length to fit)

width of workpiece

ROUTER JIG

NAIL LEVEL guide strip to each side of tip, then build jig. Measure down from jig to find lowest point. Adjust bit projection to cut slightly deeper than the low point.

START ROUTER and push through jig. Make passes about ⅝ in. apart, sliding jig along as you go. The difference between the old and new is apparent in the half-finished surface shown.

Recorder repairs you can make

WEAK BATTERIES can cause more problems than you think. Replace them frequently and in sets—not just one at a time. Be sure the cells are correctly inserted according to the polarity markings inside the case.

■ CASSETTE RECORDERS may seem complicated, but actually they're basically simple. They all work pretty much alike, and in most cases their parts are readily accessible. Before you throw up your hands at a balky machine, try these quick and easy fixits. Chances are, they'll get an ailing machine back in shape without your having to resort to major repairs.

Weak or dead batteries in a portable recorder cause more problems than you may realize. This may sound a little silly—like checking to see if the power cord is plugged in on a dead appliance—but it's such a simple thing it's often overlooked—just like the power cord that *did* unknowingly pull loose. Run-down batteries cause variations in tape speed that produce "wow" sounds or make the musicians seem to be playing in a tub of molasses.

If the drive spindles turn normally when the machine is empty, but stop or slow down the minute you insert a cassette, this generally indicates the batteries are weak—just strong enough to drive the spindles freely, but unable to take the added load of the tape.

If your recorder has a 117-volt a.c. adapter, make a quick check by switching to this. If it performs well on house current, the batteries are obviously the culprit. In replacing them, change the whole set—batteries in series wear out about evenly. Also make sure the battery terminals are clean and make firm contact.

When the machine won't budge with a tape inserted, but purrs along smoothly when you take it out, the cassette itself may be at fault. The tiny tape inside sometimes snarls or spills so it runs sluggishly or jams the drive mechanism. The answer here is to try several other cassettes. If the machine checks out okay on these, you can blame the first cassette. But don't throw it away.

A snarled tape can often be cleared by running it rapidly back and forth. Try to get it to move on "Fast Forward," then reverse it and run it backward on "Rewind." Do this several times, then see if it will run through at normal forward speed. If your recorder doesn't have a Fast Forward, rewind the cassette in one direction, then flip it over and rewind it the other way. This has

TO REACH THE TOP SIDE of the mechanism, remove the screws holding the chassis frame to the case, then carefully lift the chassis out and turn it over. Watch out for fine wires that may run to battery contacts in the case.

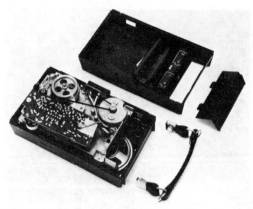

REMOVING THE BOTTOM of the case usually exposes the underside of the chassis, motor and flywheel (above). It may also release the handle and other small parts. Note how they fit together to facilitate reassembly. Using a cotton swab dipped in alcohol, clean oil and grime off the motor pulley and flywheel (below). Such dirt can cause belt slippage, varying the drive speed.

the same effect as running the tape forward at fast speed.

The next most common cassette troubles are the periodic buildup of magnetism on the heads and the dirt and grime that collect on the heads and in the drive mechanism. Dirt on the heads prevents the tape from making good contact, clogs the delicate head gaps and quickly reduces sound quality. Oily grime on the capstan, pulleys and drive belts causes tape slippage that, like weak batteries, results in wow, erratic tape speed and annoying fluctuations in musical pitch.

Cleaning and demagnetizing the heads can be done on most recorders without dismantling them. This should be done at least twice a year—more if you give your machine heavy use. The heads pick up magnetic charges as the tape moves past which interfere with proper recording and playback of magnetic signals on the tape, resulting in poor sound reproduction.

Small demagnetizing tools cost a few dollars at electronics and hi-fi shops. You plug the tool into 117-volt a.c. and move its tip back and forth a few times across each head. Keep the tool from actually touching the heads to avoid damaging the delicate surfaces. The tip should just brush lightly by them. Be sure no prerecorded tapes are lying nearby as they may be demagnetized and erased accidentally.

For cleaning the heads, you can use ordinary denatured alcohol or special solvent sold for the job. Apply it gently with a cotton swab, as shown in the accompanying photos. Particles of mag-

HEADS CAN BE CLEANED with a special solvent or ordinary denatured alcohol. Wipe them alternately with wet and dry swabs until no traces of dirt remain.

netic oxide rub off the tape during playing and must be thoroughly cleaned out of the tiny head gaps or they'll clog them. A silicone head lubricant is also available to provide a smooth, gliding surface for the tape. Other aids you can buy include test tapes for checking on various performance characteristics and head-cleaning tapes that do the cleaning job for you. The latter are handy, but should not replace an occasional thorough hand cleaning.

For inside cleaning, you'll need to remove the mechanism from its housing. In some models, the chassis is exposed by removing a cover. In others, the chassis lifts out of the enclosure from the top. Be careful on the more intricate autoreversing and changer models not to damage the delicate machinery. Portable machines are much simpler. Their housings are usually in two shell-like halves. You remove the bottom shell first, exposing the underside of the chassis. Then you take the chassis out of the top shell and turn it over to reach parts on the upper side. Battery contacts are usually in the form of springy clips that can be slipped off plastic posts to free the chassis.

Using swabs and solvent, clean all pulleys, capstans, pinch rollers, spindle hubs, drive belts and other moving parts. Gently check the belts for good tension. Replace any that are loose. Exact replacements can be ordered through hi-fi dealers or the maker of your particular recorder. But don't attempt to open a machine still in warranty as this will void it. Extensive repairs are best left for a trained serviceman.

PERIODIC DEMAGNETIZING of the heads is easy with a small demagnetizing tool. The tip should just brush past—but not actually touch—each head. The pinch roller should press the tape firmly against the capstan for a smooth, uniform drive. You can check the pressure by drawing a thin strip of paper between the roller and the capstan as shown below.

CLEAN UPPER PULLEYS in the same way as the lower ones with an alcohol swab. Also wipe the capstan, pinch roller and tape guides. Gently check the belt tension.

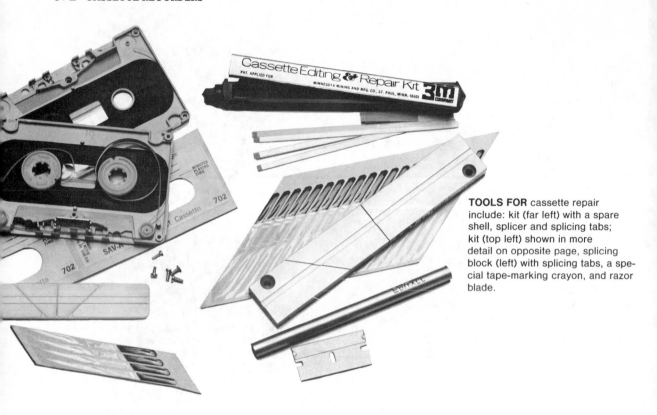

TOOLS FOR cassette repair include: kit (far left) with a spare shell, splicer and splicing tabs; kit (top left) shown in more detail on opposite page, splicing block (left) with splicing tabs, a special tape-marking crayon, and razor blade.

Snarled cassette tapes can be fixed

■ CASSETTE TAPES don't break or snarl as often as they used to—improvements in cassette construction have seen to that. But the cheaper cassettes still are often troublesome, and even the better ones cause occasional problems—invariably on recordings that simply can't be duplicated.

The most common cassette problem is the jammed cassette whose tape won't move. The cause usually is friction inside the cassette, and an uneven "pack" of tape around the cassette's internal hubs. But the cure is usually simple:

Hold the cassette three or four feet above a hard surface (such as a desktop or an uncarpeted floor), and drop the cassette so that it lands flat. Do this several times, including at least once on each side. It won't damage the cassette, and will frequently cure the jam-up.

If it doesn't, you'll have to open the cassette. If it's held together with screws (usually five small Phillips-head ones), you're in luck. Place the cassette flat and screw-side up on a table with plenty of clear working space. Carefully remove the screws, the top shell and the plastic slipsheet inside. If your luck still holds, and the tape hasn't broken or stretched, you can simply smooth it out and wind it back in place.

There seems to be no good way to open welded cassettes; the best we've found is to stand the cassette up on its broad edge (the one through which the tape shows), rest a screwdriver on the seam in one corner (between the tab pushout and the right edge), hammer the screwdriver till the seam opens, then force the screwdriver down the edge to break the rest of the seam. Repeat this on the other side and, if need be, along the back seam.

Tool no. 1: the spare-parts kit

If you've just had to blast open a welded cassette, or if parts of your cassette are broken or missing, or if the problem is due to such corner-cutting as using fixed plastic pins instead of tiny rollers to guide the tape, you'll need a spare-parts kit.

These kits are actually spare cassettes with everything but tape in them. There are two shells, two plastic hubs, the slip-sheets which prevent friction and static electricity from building up inside the cassette, tiny teflon rollers and stainless-steel pins to hold them in place, pressure-pad assemblies, and metal shields—plus, usually, a cassette splicer and splicing tape.

As needed, you can replace missing or defective parts from one of these kits, or lift the entire tape pack and takeup hub from the old shell to the new one. If that's the case, thread the tape carefully around the rollers, inside the plastic tape guides and in front of the pressure pad behind the tape window at the cassette's edge.

Tool no. 2: the 3M repair kit

If the only problem is broken tape, you don't have to open the cassette up—not since handy cassette editing and repair kits are on the market. The kits include pliable plastic wands with sticky ends with which you can fish down into the cassette shell to pick up the tape end—usually after several tries—and bring it out for splicing (more on that shortly). Once the repair's complete, you fit one end of the kit's case into one of the tape hubs to wind up the slack tape you've pulled out for splicing.

Tool no. 3: the splicing block

Splicing any tape requires a device to cut broken tape ends neatly and to hold those ends in alignment while the splicing tape is applied and trimmed. There are lots of splicers around for cassette tape (regular-tape splicers can't be used—cassette tape's too narrow), some with two arms that hold the tape while a third arm comes down to trim the tape ends or the splicing tape, others are simple blocks with channels that hold the tape while you cut and trim with razor blades. The weight keeps it steady (you can also screw it down), its slot is deeply undercut to hold the tape securely, its aluminum construction keeps razor blades from widening the cutting slits and its splicing tape tabs are very easy to apply.

When splicing, always be sure the tape's shiniest side is up, and that neither end is twisted. Then overlap the ends by half an inch or so, make a diagonal cut with a razor blade (or your cutter's built-in splicer, if it has one), remove the loose ends, butt the clean-cut ends together, and attach the tape. Trim away any bits of splicing tape which overlap the edges of the tape; overhead-arm splicers do this for you, but with blocks, you have to run your razor blade along the undercut lip of the tape-holding slot to do it.

The kit (photos above) includes strips that fish broken tape ends out of the cassette shell, a splicing block to repair broken ends, and a winder to take up slack in the tape after the completion of repairs.

CEILINGS now become an important part of the decorating scheme instead of being plain overheads that go unnoticed.

THIS tile is a good example of the new decorator tiles available. It features a textured motif on a textured base.

Ceiling tile installation

■ DO YOU HAVE a ceiling problem? If so, there's a good chance that you can find a solution through the use of ceiling tile.

Because of the simple installation systems available today, you can do the work yourself and end up with results equal to anything you might pay to have done. The work is simple and straightforward, requiring no special tools or techniques. In most cases, you can do a room from start to finish over a weekend.

Which of the following problems do you have?

Noisy room. If you have a room—for example, a family room—with a noise level that is sending you out of this world, install an acoustical ceiling. The little bouncing decibels won't ricochet off acoustical tiles, and the noise level will be appreciably lower.

Cracked, damaged ceiling. If the thought of

THE PLANKED ceiling is another new design for tiled ceilings. This one is oak planks of random width and length in the color of natural wood.

THE SQUARES are accentuated in this ceiling with rough fabric-surfaced tiles. Big variety of designs gives unlimited decorating latitude.

renovating a cracked, damaged ceiling by replastering or installing new drywall is scaring you, relax and check your dealer for a ceiling tile design you like. You can cover the old ceiling in a day.

High ceilings. Do you have one of those marvelous old houses with 10 or 12-ft. ceilings? If so, you are wasting money pumping heat into all those cubic feet of empty space above the standard 8-ft. height. The logical way to improve the room dimensions and save on energy is to suspend a new ceiling at the standard level.

Dull, uninteresting room. You've had painted walls and painted ceilings and a dull, unspectacular room for a long time, and now you'd like to give it some pizzazz. There are scores of ceiling-tile answers for this problem. If you have bypassed tile in the past because you didn't like the "tile look," go back to the store and look again. In addition to an amazing range of textured and sculptured tile surfaces, you'll now find designs in cork, wood paneling, marble and wood planking. With these available, you can take off in dozens of interior-design directions.

Insulation problems. Insulation is one problem you shouldn't try to solve with ceiling tiles, and it is mentioned here only to save you from spending money on an application that will be ineffective. First, you shouldn't install insulation between two heated rooms, such as a family room in the basement and the kitchen upstairs. You really want an exchange of warm air between those rooms. Second, the R value of ceiling tiles is too low to make much difference. And third, true insulating panels, such as those made of glass fibers, are more effective when installed in walls and roofs, in normal insulation installations, rather than in a ceiling.

Room light problems. If you have rooms that are dark or need a new lighting treatment, once again, look to a tiled ceiling. The majority of ceiling tile systems include a variety of matching translucent panels which can be intermingled with the tiles. Result: Built-in lighting, strategically placed to provide an even light over the entire area.

FIRST STEP in installing a tile system is to nail metal tracks to the old ceiling. Special nails come with the kit.

NEXT, POSITION the tile against the track and insert its tongue in the groove of the previously installed tile. System works for planks and tiles.

A new ceiling. If you are adding a room, or finishing a basement or attic area, you need to install a ceiling. One way is to use drywall. Another is to put up a tile ceiling. The tile installation is quicker and easier, and allows for easier light-fixture installation.

What's involved?

To install a tile ceiling in your home you first must select and buy the tile, along with the installation system which goes with it. Here is some buying information:

Tiles: You can purchase tiles in standard 12x12-in. tiles, 24x24-in. panels, and in 24x48-in. panels. Some systems may even offer other sizes, such as 12x48-in. Which size should you buy? In part, this question will be answered by the design that appeals to you the most. The larger panels offer a wider variety of unusual designs. Another consideration might be that you can finish a room faster with larger panels because there are fewer pieces of suspension track and fewer panels to put up in any given room.

The biggest and perhaps most difficult decision will come in deciding which of the wide array of designs you want. Your major consideration in

this decision should be the use and decor of the room. Some of the designs are formal and elegant—hardly the thing for a child's room or the laundry area. Others are simple and not intended to catch the eye. Would you like the majesty of a marble ceiling? In the right room, a marble ceiling would provide great eye appeal and a lot of conversation.

Or perhaps you might consider a ceiling of wood. You can find a variety of wood effects including square oak panels and oak or pine planking designs. If the room is already paneled or you intend to panel it, you can install a ceiling to match or to provide a warm contrast.

When inspecting tile designs, remember that not all ceiling tiles absorb sound. If sound control is one reason for installing a tile ceiling, then be sure the design you select is made to absorb sound. Many designs have virtually no acoustical effect. Those that are acoustically designed are clearly labeled, so check the label before buying.

If you are planning to install a tile ceiling in a kitchen or bathroom, check the labels and literature for information on cleaning. Some wood fiber tiles cannot be washed, only vacuumed. Others can be sponged with mild soap and water. Some acoustical tiles can be painted a number of

SPECIAL CLIP snaps on the track and slides over the tile lip. Clips are hidden when tiles are up, and only one clip per tile is needed.

Tile systems

There are three basic systems for installing ceiling tile. In the first, the tiles are cemented directly to the present ceiling. In the second, wood or metal furring strips are attached to the ceiling, and the tile is either stapled to the furring strips or supported by them, depending on the system. In the third, the entire ceiling is suspended on a metal frame that hangs beneath the original ceiling suspended by wires.

There are a lot of variations on these systems, since each maker has developed his own version. In simple suspension systems, you can use any maker's tile as long as the tile panels are the right size and cut square at the edges. In simple furring-strip installations, you can install any flanged tile, since you staple through the flange into the furring strip. But when you look at any system employing clips or other special devices, be careful because these are a part of an integrated system that probably won't interface with any other system.

The important point to remember is: Be sure to buy a whole system—tiles and suspension parts—or carefully check to see that the tiles and other parts you buy will mix. Note that one manufacturer may make two or three systems, and

times and still retain their sound absorbency, others can be painted a few times, and still others cannot be painted at all.

If you are putting a ceiling in the kitchen, figure that you'll have to clean it often. Even a good exhaust fan won't prevent airborne grease from being deposited on the kitchen walls and ceiling, so cleaning is a real necessity. In bathrooms, steamy showers cause moisture to form on the ceiling, and the moisture deposits minerals which will have to be cleaned eventually.

Other rooms, such as bedrooms or living and dining rooms, get dirty at a much slower rate, and the dirt is easier to clean off. All of this means that any tile put up in "dirty" rooms such as the kitchen should be washable, while tile in the other rooms probably will look good with simple vacuuming and damp-cloth wiping.

One final word on design. Some tile systems are designed to emphasize the seams where the tiles join. In others, the metal parts of the installation system show as a part of the ceiling design. Others are made so that you see no seam or metal at all. Again, the choice is yours. But if you are allergic to the "tile look," the no-seam systems should appeal. In many of these, only you will know that the ceiling is tiled.

ANOTHER METHOD for installing tiles on a sound ceiling is to staple them in place. Use long staples and do not staple to damaged spots.

CEILING SYSTEM uses tracks nailed to or hung below joists. Most systems are similar, but fittings are seldom interchangeable.

ONCE THE TRACKS are up, cross members are installed between them. Tile systems generally are light in weight and easy to install.

these systems may not mix—so don't buy by manufacturer's name alone. Look for the name of the system and buy everything in that one system.

System considerations. The system you select in part will be determined by the problem you are trying to solve. If you are putting up a ceiling as a finishing touch in a basement playroom, then you'll find floor-to-ceiling height a prime consideration. Most basement ceilings are less than 8 feet from the floor to the bottom of the floor joists overhead, and you'll want your ceiling to take up as little space as possible. In this case, the furring-strip method is best. You can use kiln-dried furring strips, to which you staple the ceiling tiles, or nail up metal tracks which support the tiles.

If you are lowering a high ceiling, you will need a suspension system, consisting of metal tracks that support the tiles. The tracks usually are suspended by wires at a number of points across the room. The wires attach to screw eyes you screw into the old ceiling.

To cover a damaged ceiling, you also should use the furring-strip method. In this case, you nail either wood or metal furring strips through

the old ceiling to the joists above.

If you are putting a new tile ceiling over a sound old ceiling, then the easiest method is to cement the tiles directly to the old ceiling. You put a small dab of cement on each corner of the tile and add another dab in the middle. Then you squish the tile against the old ceiling and slide it into contact with adjacent tiles you have already put up.

Tile installation

You'll get a complete set of instructions with the tile system you buy. Follow the step-by-step operations as directed, but here are some general points.

Furring strips. When buying 1x2 lumber for use as furring strips, ask for kiln-dried wood and select straight unwarped pieces. Warped or bent strips will result in an uneven ceiling. The instructions with your tiles will tell you to establish centerlines across the room in each direction, and put up furring strips beginning at the center and working towards the walls.

Locate the ceiling joists and nail through the furring strips into these. The furring strips are

WITH THE SUPPORT members in place, installing the ceiling is just a matter of placing the tiles on the flanges of the framework.

For suspended ceilings, screw eyes are installed at intervals in the present ceiling, and a wall molding is nailed up at the height of the new ceiling. The main runners which support the ceiling tiles are suspended from these screw eyes by hanger wires. Once the runners are suspended in place, the tiles or panels are laid in on their tile-supporting flanges, beginning at one corner of the room and progressing from there. Some systems use cross tees and some do not.

The installation of any of these systems proceeds quickly, so there is seldom any problem in doing a room in a day or over a weekend.

One final note. Order your tile delivered several days before you intend to put it up. Open the boxes and keep them in the house. This permits them to adjust to the atmospheric conditions of the house. Most tiles expand and contract slightly as the moisture content of the air increases and decreases. This also is the reason why most tile manufacturers instruct you not to press tiles together too tightly as you mount them. If they are slightly loose, they have room to expand.

nailed in rows located far enough apart so each tile is supported on two sides. You may have to shim out some furring strips to level them.

Tiles are attached to furring strips with ⁹⁄₁₆-in. staples driven by a staple gun. Don't staple tiles to drywall or plaster surfaces. They won't hold. If you use metal-channel furring strips, you also will mount a wall molding around the room to support the tiles at the wall.

After the furring is up, begin putting up tiles in one corner of the room. With wood furring, staple the first tile, then fit the flanges of the next tile into it. Push the second tile into a close fit, be sure the edges of the tiles are squarely aligned, then staple the second tile. With metal furring, slide the first tile into position, then insert the cross tee which locks the tile into place. (The use of cross tees varies with the system.)

You seldom will have the number of tiles in a row come out even, and the last tile in the row must be cut to fit. Follow the instructions for tile cutting, since they may vary with the tile material. Two things are important. Measure carefully before cutting, and cut carefully to make neat, square edges.

ELEGANCE is the word for this formal dining-room ceiling. This design is a far cry from the plain tiled ceilings of the past.

Simulated ceiling beams— easy to install

■ SIMULATED "hand-hewn" wall and ceiling beams offer one of the easiest ways to add decorator elegance to an interior remodeling job. Available prefinished and ready-to-install, the easy-to-work beams can even be cut with a bread knife. They're applied using adhesive, nails or a clip-system designed by the manufacturer. Unfinished beams—which can be stained or painted as you prefer—are available by special order.

Ceiling beams come in 8 to 18-ft. lengths (in 2-ft. graduations); wall beams are sold in 8, 12 and 16-ft. lengths. The accessories available for use with the beams include matching corner braces with 45° mitered ends, recommended adhesive for best results, matching stains to disguise any marks, and simulated hand-hammered brackets for covering beam joints.

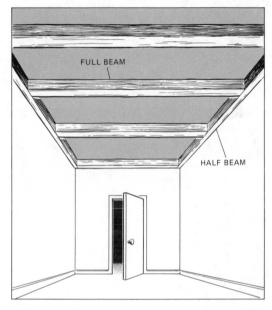

BEFORE CUTTING any material, you would be wise to make a scale drawing of the room, indicating beam locations. If the room is long and narrow, run the beams crosswise to provide the illusion of a wide room. The apron around the room, at the wall-ceiling angle, is created by using half-beams to make it seem that the other half is *in the wall*.

WARMTH AND CHARM of 200-year-old beams is captured with replicas of expanded urethane.

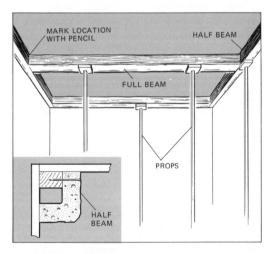

SNUG BUTT JOINTS are assured if you cut beams one at a time and temporarily prop them in position with thin sticks wedged between floor and beam (use block of wood under beam to prevent damage). To install half-beam apron permanently along ceiling line, first nail furring strip in the angle, then use adhesive and 8d finishing nails.

A TABLE SAW equipped with a fine-tooth combination or plywood blade is ideal for cutting urethane beams. If you don't have this equipment, the cutting will still be easy with a sharp, crosscut handsaw (and square)—it just takes slightly longer. To rip a U-shape beam, run it upside down (above) for safety and sufficient blade protection.

TECHNIQUES for attaching plastic beams: When using self-sticking beams (above), you just peel off tab and stick into place. If installing beams to be positioned between joists (drawing below), strike centerlines where beams will be applied, and then install suitable-width furring strips using toggle bolts. Beams are then secured to the furring strips with adhesive and 8d finishing nails. When applying adhesive with a caulking gun (photo, below), add it sparingly down the center of the beam surfaces to avoid squeeze-out on ceiling or wall when you press beams in place. Finally, set finishing nails, fill heads.

BEAM CAN ALSO BE RIPPED with a sabre saw after tacking a wood strip to plastic for use as fence.

WHEN CROSSCUTTING, if blade won't cut beam with one pass, make initial cut and turn over to complete.

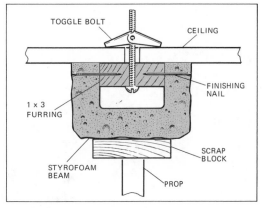

TOGGLE BOLT

CEILING

1 x 3 FURRING

FINISHING NAIL

STYROFOAM BEAM

SCRAP BLOCK

PROP

BEFORE BEAMS were installed, living-room ceiling looked as uninteresting as any other.

AFTER BEAMS went up, they served to direct attention to fireplace area, tied room together.

Antique ceiling beams

■ YOU CAN COMPLEMENT your colonial decor with a beamed ceiling. Although new foam-type beams are good reproductions, you may want to carve out your own.

To make them, you'll need rough-sawn, non-dimensional stock measuring about 4x6 in. Sometimes you can get this stock at little or no cost. The beams shown were flatcar dunnage (pine) salvaged from a railroad siding. The railroad people were happy to have the timbers hauled away. If you have no local railroad freight

SURPLUS PICK-MATTOCK is rough-ground into an adz, using portable grinder. Bevel is on the inside.

CUTTING EDGE is honed razor-sharp to insure fine cuts and ripples that mark the work of an adz.

PLUGS ARE CUT from side that butts against ceiling, and are used to fill holes that came with timber.

COATED WITH GLUE, the plugs are then driven into enlarged nail holes before adzing begins.

EASIEST METHOD of adzing is to straddle raised beam. Use workstop or clamps to prevent movement.

TO MAKE UP TIMBERS for long spans, beveled lap splices are cut on ends of beam to be joined.

yard or other source of cheap nondimensional stock, you can substitute dimensional lumber.

Make your own adz

Though the adz is a tool that has been in use for centuries—it was the only known method of dressing lumber—it is not easy to come by now. (Chances are if you do locate one, the price will be high.) Your first problem is how to achieve an adzed look on your beams. An ax, hatchet or spoon chisel doesn't give satisfactory results in getting the look you want. The obvious answer is to make your own adz.

The dictionary describes an adz as a cutting tool having a thin arching blade set at right angles to the handle. You can start with a used pick-mattock (the mattock blade fits the description) at a surplus store for a couple of bucks. Then, grind a razor-sharp edge on the tool.

How to use an adz

To hew, straddle a timber that is held securely

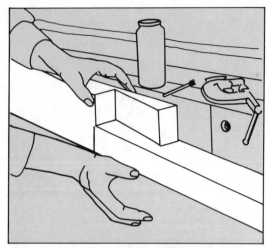

BEVELED SPLICES are checked to insure fit, then assembled, using glue, lagscrews and dowel-plugs.

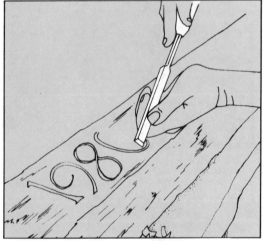

DATE CARVED in main beam is optional but adds to realism. Or, use the year you bought the house.

by workstops on the floor. Use short, well-aimed strokes down and toward you in the curvature of the blade. Your arms and the handle act as the radius. The blade is worked across the width of the beam stroke by stroke, removing stock several inches long and wide with each chop.

This is tricky. An angled stroke, or a hard chop that strikes a knot, can glance off and give a painful and serious cut to your shin. To avoid this, many pros working at a fast pace stand in wooden nail kegs to protect their legs. Your safest bet is to work slowly, always making certain the cutting edge strikes *with* the grain on each stroke. When working over a knot, use much shorter strokes or use a chisel.

Having a shorter handle than an adz, the mattock-adz shown is best handled by elevating the workpiece and following the safety rules mentioned above. Do one side from end to end, then rotate the timber 90° and do the next side. Always work with the grain; cutting against it leaves deep, ugly gashes. Your first efforts may result in cutting sharp, jagged splinters. These can be removed with a hand chisel.

Installing the beams

The room where the beams shown were installed has a wide entry. A wide beam was run across the opening. The long-spanning beams (actually joists in old construction) are at right angles to the heavy beam. They simply butt the walls at one end and are let into notches cut in the heavy beam at the other. The notches are cut extra deep so the beam can slide in as you swing

BEAM END is chiseled out to receive wall-knee support. Kerfs made with a power saw speed this step.

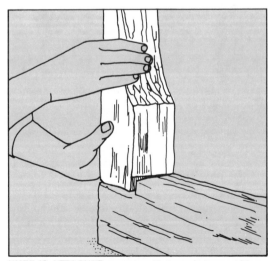

KNEE IS ATTACHED permanently to main beam with glue and dowels before the beam is installed.

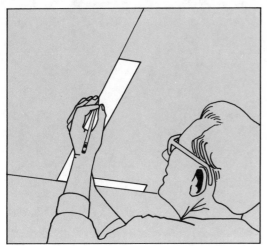

CEILING JOIST CENTER LINE is established on both sides of room and chalkline is snapped across.

PREDRILLED BEAM is positioned over chalkline, held fast by T-support wedged with shims, then bolted.

WALL KNEE, attached to beam, is positioned against the wall and drilled for lagscrews that will hold it.

the far end up, letting the beam clear the wall.

Installation goes a lot faster if you have some help hefting the beams into position. And it's worth the time it takes to build a T-support, which, with several wedges and a helper, makes installation comparatively easy.

Predrill and counterbore all beams for lagscrews and bolts while still in the workshop. Then lay out beam locations on the ceiling with ruler and chalkline. When a beam is positioned and wedged firmly in place, drill pilot holes into the joists to receive the lagscrews. After the beam is securely fastened, the shimmed T-support can be removed safely.

For extra support, you can bolt knees to wall studs beneath each end of the heavy beam. About 18 in. long, the ones shown were found—as is—alongside the dunnage beams in the railroad yard. They had been discarded after serving as chocks under a large cast-iron boiler brought in on a flat car.

The beams shown were finished with walnut stain and two coats of semigloss varnish. This part of the job goes a lot faster if you do the staining and first varnish coat before the beams are in place. Then it's a simple matter to touch up the few spots that might get bruised during installation and apply the second coat of varnish.

POST SUPPORTING BEAM stays put until all bolts are turned home. Knee is fastened to wall next.

Tough cuts with your chain saw made easy

GETTING yourself and your chain saw up a tree, and felling limbs safely, takes know-how. This treeman is trimming small branches before cutting a heavy limb.

■ THERE ARE A NUMBER of reasons why a homeowner may have to remove a tree in crowded quarters. Perhaps it, or some of its branches, are so close to the house that it presents a hazard during storms. Or maybe some heavy, dead limbs pose a threat and should be removed. And, nowadays, trees that cast shadows where we plan to put solar collectors must go.

Before you can do anything, you must get up in the tree with a saw. Surprisingly, you can accomplish this and still have your hands free for sawing by rigging up a rope saddle and a treeman's knot.

This rigging allows you to safely control your up and down movements in the tree. If you slip, or a limb breaks under your weight, you won't come tumbling down, but just dangle until you can regain your footing. To free your hands for sawing, put your body weight in the saddle and brace yourself with your feet against the tree trunk or limbs.

The big secret to taking down limbs, or the entire tree, is to do it *a little bit at a time.* Saw off sections small enough to be easily handled and let down by rope. It takes time, but it's safe.

You need at least one other person on the ground to handle the ropes, and you need at least three strong ropes in good condition. Buy new ropes if there is any doubt about the condition of the ropes you own.

All ropes should be more than twice as long as the height at which you will be working in the tree. Rope lengths of 100 feet will handle most tree work. They should be free of knots and kinks and the frayed ends should be taped, not braided or knotted. Knots will catch in a tree crotch and prevent you from pulling the rope through.

One good way to test a rope for strength is to tie one end to your car's rear bumper and the other around a tree trunk. Ease the car forward until the rope is taut, then apply a steady pulling pressure. Look for areas of excess stretching. This is also a handy way to take the kinks out of a rope or to take the stretch out of a new rope.

The most important rope is the one which will be supporting you, and with which you will tie your saddle. This should be at least ⅝-inch-diameter manila hemp rope—¾-inch rope would be even better. Nylon or other synthetic fiber ropes are too slippery for good control with the treeman's knot.

The second rope is the one you tie to the limb to be sawed off for lowering. It should be strong enough for the weight, so use ½-inch rope.

The third rope is used to haul your saw up after you have placed yourself in working position, or to swing branches out of the way of obstructions. A strong ¼-inch rope is fine.

Working up in a tree with a roaring chain saw can be extremely dangerous unless you have absolute control over the saw, your own movements and the movement of the limb you want to drop. If, at any time, you have doubt about your ability to do all three safely with a chain saw, by all means use a hand saw. At any rate, for best control, use only a lightweight chain saw.

If you try to use a chain saw, be sure to heed these safety hints:

■ Wear a hard hat, and if using a loud saw, ear protection.

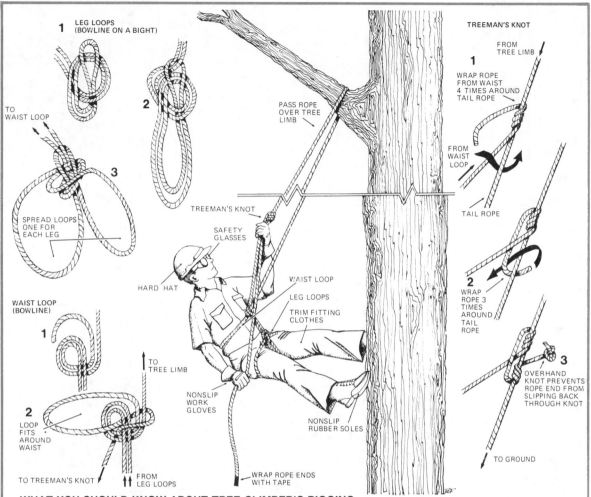

1 LEG LOOPS (BOWLINE ON A BIGHT)

2

TO WAIST LOOP

3

SPREAD LOOPS ONE FOR EACH LEG

PASS ROPE OVER TREE LIMB

TREEMAN'S KNOT

SAFETY GLASSES

HARD HAT

WAIST LOOP

LEG LOOPS

TRIM FITTING CLOTHES

NONSLIP WORK GLOVES

NONSLIP RUBBER SOLES

WAIST LOOP (BOWLINE)

1

TO TREE LIMB

2 LOOP FITS AROUND WAIST

TO TREEMAN'S KNOT

FROM LEG LOOPS

WRAP ROPE ENDS WITH TAPE

TREEMAN'S KNOT

1 FROM TREE LIMB

WRAP ROPE FROM WAIST 4 TIMES AROUND TAIL ROPE

FROM WAIST LOOP

TAIL ROPE

2 WRAP ROPE 3 TIMES AROUND TAIL ROPE

3 OVERHAND KNOT PREVENTS ROPE END FROM SLIPPING BACK THROUGH KNOT

TO GROUND

WHAT YOU SHOULD KNOW ABOUT TREE CLIMBER'S RIGGING

THE KNOTS shown here make a safe saddle. You can become familiar with them through on-the-ground practice. They must be tied so they do not slip. Otherwise, they will cause the rope to tighten around you.

The saddle should have a snug, comfortable fit when your entire weight is on it. If the ropes bite into your skin too much, wrap them with rags or leather for padding. When you get to the site, it's a good idea to retie the knots a couple of times to get a good fit.

The saddle must be tied before you can pass the rope over the support limb. To start, measure off about 12 feet from one end of the rope and fold it back on itself. Begin tying your leg loops about three feet from the bend on the doubled end, using a bowline on a bight. Then proceed to the waist loop and the treeman's knot.

After passing the rope over the support limb, be certain that you test out your saddle and treeman's knot before you begin your climb.

PASS ROPE over strong, high limb after tying saddle and treeman's knots.

BE SURE to test your safety rigging near the ground before you climb tree.

TREEMAN'S KNOT suspends you safely, yet allows you to go up or down.

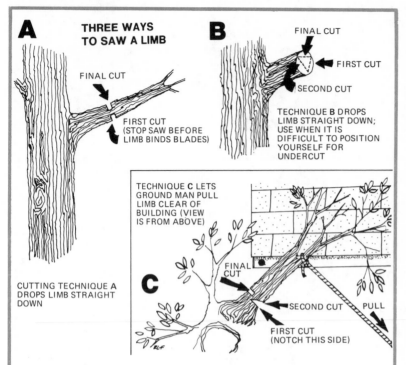

A THREE WAYS TO SAW A LIMB

FINAL CUT

FIRST CUT (STOP SAW BEFORE LIMB BINDS BLADES)

CUTTING TECHNIQUE A DROPS LIMB STRAIGHT DOWN

B

FINAL CUT

FIRST CUT

SECOND CUT

TECHNIQUE B DROPS LIMB STRAIGHT DOWN; USE WHEN IT IS DIFFICULT TO POSITION YOURSELF FOR UNDERCUT

C

TECHNIQUE C LETS GROUND MAN PULL LIMB CLEAR OF BUILDING (VIEW IS FROM ABOVE)

FINAL CUT

SECOND CUT

PULL

FIRST CUT (NOTCH THIS SIDE)

CUTTING technique (A) shows standard approach to dropping limb straight down from tree. Method (B) lets you make the final cut from above. All cuts should be in the same plane. Technique (C) enables the man on the ground to swing the limb clear of an obstruction or house.

HOW TO THROW ROPE OVER A LIMB

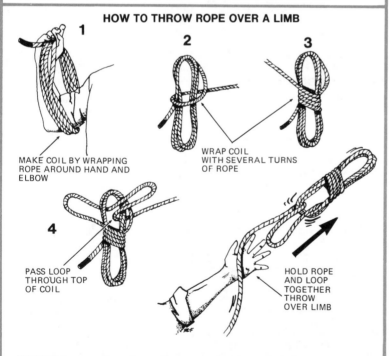

1 MAKE COIL BY WRAPPING ROPE AROUND HAND AND ELBOW

2 WRAP COIL WITH SEVERAL TURNS OF ROPE

3

4 PASS LOOP THROUGH TOP OF COIL

HOLD ROPE AND LOOP TOGETHER THROW OVER LIMB

MAKING a rope coil, as shown above, provides sufficient weight for making toss—and lets rope unwind as it comes down. Excess rope should be loosely coiled on the ground so it won't restrict the airborne coil.

HOW TO USE YOUR CHAIN SAW IN A TREE

1 GROUND MAN lifts saw to working position, using rope tied to saw's balance point.

2 BRACE SAW in crotch for starting. *Don't maneuver with saw running.*

3 TO MAKE CUT, place your body weight in the saddle and brace yourself firmly with your feet.

4 FINAL limb-dropping cut is made while you're safely out of the way (preferably above) of the falling limb.

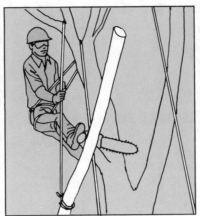

5 TO AVOID DAMAGE, tree man can aid ground man by using guide rope tied at balance point to help control limb.

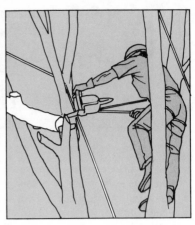

6 FELLING larger branches can cause the tree to sway. Be prepared for this sudden movement by bracing yourself.

■ Check out your saw on the ground. Make sure it starts easily, and that the chain does not turn when the engine is idling.

■ Up in the tree, don't start the engine until you have positioned yourself to make the cut, and switch off the engine the moment the limb drops. Don't try to maneuver in the tree with the saw running.

■ Brace the saw firmly in a tree fork when you start it.

■ Keep a safety rope tied to the saw handle at its balance point. Have the other end of the safety rope secured or controlled by the ground man. Keep enough slack in the rope so that if you drop the saw, it will remain suspended several feet below any position you might slip to, yet not present any danger to someone on the ground. This way, if you lose control, you can drop the saw to use your hands to steady yourself without damaging the saw.

■ Be sure the safety rope on the saw and your own safety rope are away from the path of any movement of the limb rope when the limb drops or swings.

Always make sure your safety rope is properly attached and supported by a limb sound enough to hold your weight.

You can use an extension ladder to climb up into the branches. However, you may want it removed after you are in the tree to clear the way for lowering branches.

To get your safety rope across a suitable branch, it can be tossed over, using the method illustrated, or you can climb the ladder and put it over by hand. Where possible, the rope should be passed all the way around the trunk, using the crotch as a stop rather than a support. Be sure that the tree crotch is not so tight it prevents the rope from being pulled through easily.

Tie your saddle in one end of the rope and attach it to the tail rope, using the treeman's knot. The knot should be only a foot or so from your saddle knots, within easy reach of your hand.

Always test your saddle and treeman's knots before going up in the tree. You can do this by suspending yourself just above the ground.

Trimming hints

There is no standard method for trimming a tree. Generally, trimmers start at the top and work down, dislodging caught branches as they descend. However, you may want to get some of the larger lower branches out of the way first.

When you saw off a branch, leave a stub one or two feet long to aid you in your climbing and rope handling. It can be cut off on your final descent if the entire tree is not to be taken down.

Remember, too, it's easy to underestimate the weight of a large limb, with all its twigs and leaves. It can be a very dangerous force. So, first cut off as many outer branches from the limb as possible and take the limb down in sections.

If you saw off a fairly large limb, the tree is relieved of considerable weight. This can cause the entire tree to sway back and forth quite violently. You must anticipate this and be prepared to switch off your chain saw immediately, and position it safely, while you brace yourself against the swaying.

Always leave a few feet of slack in the limb rope when you tie it off. There should be enough slack to let the limb drop below the working area, yet prevent it from coming down far enough to damage anything below.

Chain-saw accessory box

A CASE for your chain saw and accessories saves you the time normally spent gathering screwdrivers, wrenches and oil, and makes it less likely you'll forget to bring an item along.

Cut all pieces to size. Draw a line 3½ in. from the top of all pieces B and C. (The box will be separated into lid and case at this line after assembly.) Assemble pieces A, B and C with white glue and 1½-in. ringed (annular) nails. Start with pieces A and B to form an open-ended rectangular box. Then add endpieces, making sure marked line runs unbroken around box and no nails are within 1 in. of this separating line. Clamp and let dry for 24 hours.

Saw off box top along line to separate top and case. Place chain saw in case and mark along sides B for installation of divider later (make marks 1 in. from body of saw for clearance).

To make the tool rack, use a drill to bore holes for files, and a sabre saw and chisel to fashion the

rectangular plier spaces. Draw around base of oil and lube cans on accessory rack (E). Cut out patterns with a sabre saw. Nail piece E to D.

Nail divider, then accessory rack with support to inside of box. Secure tool rack (G) with roundhead machine screws (L). Attach handles to endpieces (C), hinges to back of lid and base, and lid catch to front center. Prime and paint if desired.

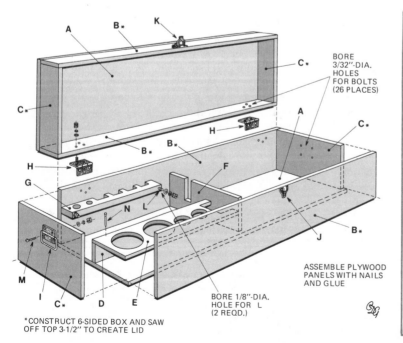

BORE 3/32''-DIA. HOLES FOR BOLTS (26 PLACES)

ASSEMBLE PLYWOOD PANELS WITH NAILS AND GLUE

BORE 1/8''-DIA. HOLE FOR L (2 REQD.)

*CONSTRUCT 6-SIDED BOX AND SAW OFF TOP 3-1/2'' TO CREATE LID

Key	No.	Size and description (use)
A	2	½ × 12 × 39'' plywood (top and bottom pieces)
B*	2	½ × 12 × 39'' plywood (front and back pieces)
C*	2	½ × 11 × 12'' plywood (sidepieces)
D	1	½ × 3 × 19'' plywood (accessory-rack support)
E	1	½ × 6 × 19'' plywood (accessory rack)
F	1	½ × 6 × 11'' plywood (divider)
G	1	¾ × 1½ × 16'' pine (tool rack)
H	2	3'' cabinet hinges
I	2	3½'' chest handles
J	1	Lid catch (bottom) and screws
K	1	Lid catch (top) and screws
L	2	No. 4 × 2¼'' rh machine screws, washers and nuts
M	20	⅛ × 1'' bolts and nuts, or to suit

MATERIALS LIST—CHAIN-SAW BOX

Misc.: White glue, 4d ringed nails as required.
*Overall dimension prior to cutting off lid.

Chain-saw maintenance tips

■ HAVING THE RIGHT saw chain on your chain saw and making sure it is kept sharp is the surest way of getting the most out of the tool. You can tell when your chain is getting dull by the size of the chips that fall at your feet. When the chain is sharp, the chips are large. A dull chain, on the other hand, spews out small, almost powdery sawdust.

A sharp chain will slide through a log with little pressure, whereas a dull chain requires excessive pressure, causing rapid wear of chain, bar and sprocket, as well as overloading of the engine. It takes only a few file strokes to keep a chain cutting efficiently, and saves you a lot of effort and aggravation later.

HOW TO SELECT THE RIGHT SAW CHAIN

Series	No.	Pitch	Gauge
MICRO CHISEL			
	20	.325″	.050″
	21	.325″	.058″
	22	⅜″	.050″
	23	⅜″	.058″
	24	⅜″	.063″
	25	.250″	.050″
Fast, versatile with semisquare cutting edges. Easy to maintain with round file. A variety of sizes to fit most saws.	26	.404″	.058″
	27	.404″	.063″
	28	.404″	.050″

No.	Pitch	Gauge	Series
102C	.250″	.050″	
45C	.354″	.058″	
12C	⅜″	.050″	**CHIPPER**
51AC	.404″	.058″	
52AC	.404″	.063″	
50C	7/16″	.050″	
61AC	7/16″	.058″	
62AC	½″	.063″	
9AC	½″	.058″	
10AC	¾″	.063″	World favorite for over 20 years. Sizes for all saws, all timber. Fast cutting, easy sharpening. A real workhorse.
11AC	¾″	.122″	
11BC	¾″	.122″	

Series	No.	Pitch	Gauge
CHISEL			
	9AL	½″	.058″
	10AL	½″	.063″
Square cutting edge never cuts same cross grain twice, removes more wood in a single pass. Requires skillful filing.			

No.	Pitch	Gauge	Series
			OREGON S-70
72D	⅜″	.050″	
73D	⅜″	.058″	
75D	⅜″	.063″	
A good chain for lightweight compact saws. Cuts fast and smooth. Easily sharpened with round file.			

Series	No.	Pitch	Gauge
SUPER CHISEL			
	50L	.404″	.050″
	51L	.404″	.058″
	52L	.404″	.063″
	50AL	.404″	.050″
	51AL	.404″	.058″
	52AL	.404″	.063″
High-cutting efficiency and smoothness in both small or big timber. Easily sharpened with round file or chisel file.			

No.	Pitch	Gauge	Series
			MICRO BIT
58AC	.404″	.058″	
59AC	.404″	.063″	
68C	7/16″	.058″	
69C	7/16″	.063″	
31C	½″	.058″	
32C	½″	.063″	
A modification of the famous chipper design. It feeds considerably faster due to its cutting-edge profile.			

Series	No.	Pitch	Gauge
OREGON 80			
	84	.404″	.063″
	85	.404″	.050″
	86	.404″	.058″
	87	.325″	.050″
	88	.325″	.058″
Fastest, smoothest chain made. Sharpens in seconds with Power Sharp system. Can also be hand-sharpened.			

GUARD LINK

Guards links are available on .325″ and ⅜″-pitch micro chisel and ⅜″ pitch S-70 (Speed guard).

Guard links provide increased protection from kickback when limbing and cutting in brushy areas. Good for use around home.

CHAIN-SAW TROUBLESHOOTING

Most chain-saw problems are caused by incorrect filing and improper chain tensions. Here are some common problems, their causes and remedies:

Cutters won't stay sharp

CAUSES	REMEDIES
1. Incorrect filing angle (blunt or sloped).	Hold file correctly. Use a file holder.
2. Depth gauges too high.	Lower the depth gauges uniformly. Use depth-gauge jointer of the correct size.
3. Cutter lengths not uniform.	File all cutters to the same length.
4. Chain not tensioned properly.	Adjust tension.
5. Abrasive wear on cutters due to dirt and sand.	File away all abrasive damage. File undamaged cutters so that they match in length.

Chain cuts roughly, chatters or grabs

CAUSES	REMEDIES
1. Incorrect filing angles: feathered edge, hook, back-sloped, top angle not 35°.	File to specifications. Use a file holder and watch carefully to see that you are holding the file in correct position.
2. Depth gauges set unevenly.	Use jointed and file uniformly.
3. Improper chain tension.	Adjust tension correctly. *Caution:* When adjusting chain tension, be sure saw is turned off. If electric, see also that it is unplugged.
4. Worn sprocket.	Replace sprocket.
5. Rivet bearings worn out due to lack of oil.	Replace chain. Always use plenty of oil when cutting.

Chain doesn't cut straight (slanted cut)

CAUSES	REMEDIES
1. Saw not supported properly.	Hold saw with both hands and guide it through the cut.
2. Cutters not filed uniformly; one side of chain uneven.	File all cutters to same length and angles.
3. Depth gauges not uniform; some being higher than others.	Lower all gauges to the same setting; use jointer of the correct size.
4. Abrasive damage to cutters on one side of chain.	File away damaged portions, then file undamaged cutters to match.
5. Bar rails worn and spread.	Have bar rebuilt or replaced.

How to break in your saw

Before starting your saw, do the following:

1. Be sure the chain is mounted correctly, facing the right direction and properly tensioned. If possible, soak the chain in oil overnight before using it.

2. Fill the chain-oil tank with chain oil and check the chain oiler button to be sure it's working.

3. If it's a gas-operated chain saw, mix fuel and oil for engine in a clean container in the proper proportion. Use chain-saw oil recommended by the manufacturer. With an electric model, you can start cutting as soon as the tool is plugged in.

To adjust tension, loosen the bar stud nuts slightly. On hard-nose bars, tighten the tension screw until you can just pull the chain around the bar by hand. Hold tip of bar up while adjusting the tension screw and tightening the stud nuts. Otherwise, the chain will loosen on the first cut. Pump the oiler a few times, while pulling the chain around the bar by hand. Then start the saw and run the chain at fast idle for two minutes—without cutting! Stop the saw and recheck the tension. To check tension, let the chain cool and pump the oiler while pulling the chain around the bar by hand. Snap the chain in the bar groove to loosen and straighten all parts. If chain is loose, readjust tension.

Start cutting—only small limbs or logs for the first half hour. Use plenty of chain oil during break-in period and watch chain tension. A new chain will "stretch" during break-in and become loose. A chain can be ruined in five minutes of cutting if it is too loose. If it is too tight or slow cutting, excess heat and friction cause rapid wear.

Type and size of saw

Most saws are of the direct-drive type today. There are gear-drive saws available, used mostly by professionals. The direct-drive saw is lighter, has fewer parts, requires less maintenance. It's easier to use, less tiring as the chain speed pulls the saw through the log without pressure. It cuts easily on any part of the bar.

For the occasional user, a lightweight saw is the best choice. Power is difficult to determine as there are no published horsepower ratings. The cubic-inch displacement of the engine is a rough guide to power—the larger the displacement, the higher the power. But there are other factors which affect the power output, such as compression, type of valving, and timing. The type of cutting chain, sprocket and guide bar are very important in the efficient use of available power. A small-pitch, fast-cutting chain running in a low-friction roller nose bar can effectively increase power.

Tips on chain-saw maintenance

■ KEEPING CHAIN SAWS running properly is a growing concern of many homeowners who are turning to wood as an alternative source of heat.

The three most important rules to follow when getting ready to use a chain saw are: 1. read the homeowner's manual and the manufacturer's instructions; 2. tighten all screws and bolts; 3. make sure the chain is properly filed.

In Photo 3, the correct procedure for mounting the chain is demonstrated. Saw owners must learn the technique when assembling a new saw for the first time. It's a good idea, however, to disassemble chain and guide bar when transporting the saw over long distances, or before storing, so it is a technique to remember. After the guide bar is mounted, straighten out any kinks in the chain and lay it out in a loop. Then, feed the chain into the grooves, as shown.

A good instruction booklet contains the information necessary to understand saw chain tension adjustment, as shown in Photo 4. Chains become warm or even hot when they are used, and you have to take this into account when tension adjustments are made.

Keeping your chain in good cutting condition makes sawing easier and safer, while prolonging the life of the saw. Photo 5 shows the first step in the sharpening process.

The raker, shown in Photos 6 and 7, controls the depth of the cut and acts like a runner guide for the cutting edge.

If you find a dirty air filter when checking the power head (Photo 9), tap the loose dirt free and then rinse out finer dirt with a nonoily petroleum solvent.

Practice chain-saw safety rules. Always maintain good balance and never work when you are tired.

1 Reading the instruction manual is one of the three most important rules in chain-saw use and maintenance. Safety hints are included.

2 Remove two hex nuts from mounting studs and remove drive-case cover. Check this area regularly to make sure nuts are tight and parts clean.

3 When assembling saw after storage, see that chain-drive tangs are set properly in guide-bar grooves. Work from sprocket to nose.

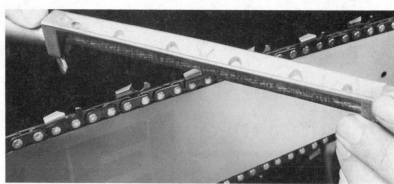

4 Lift the chain with right hand to check tension. Tension screw is then adjusted with a screwdriver. Tension should be adjusted before each use.

5 Use a file holder to maintain a 35° filing angle when filing saw teeth. Holder also keeps file at correct height. Keep file level and stroke in one direction only.

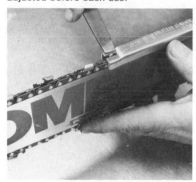

6 Use a depth-gauge jointer to true up chain's depth gauge (rakers). Fit jointer over the chain with slot toward bar nose, and file flush.

7 Viewing guide bar and chain in Photo 6 from the other side, the front side of the raker is then rounded over for a good sliding action.

8 Pull starter rope to check for proper recoil-spring action. Spring adjusts easily if necessary. Keep the air intake louvers clean.

9 Start power-head maintenance with a check of the air filter. Make sure filter and area around carburetor are clean. Seat filter properly.

10 Screwdriver points to an area near combustion cylinder where carbon accumulation may occur. Remove muffler and clean away carbon.

11 Check the sparkplug first when starting troubles occur, as a fouled plug is usually the cause. Clean plug by brushing or scraping.

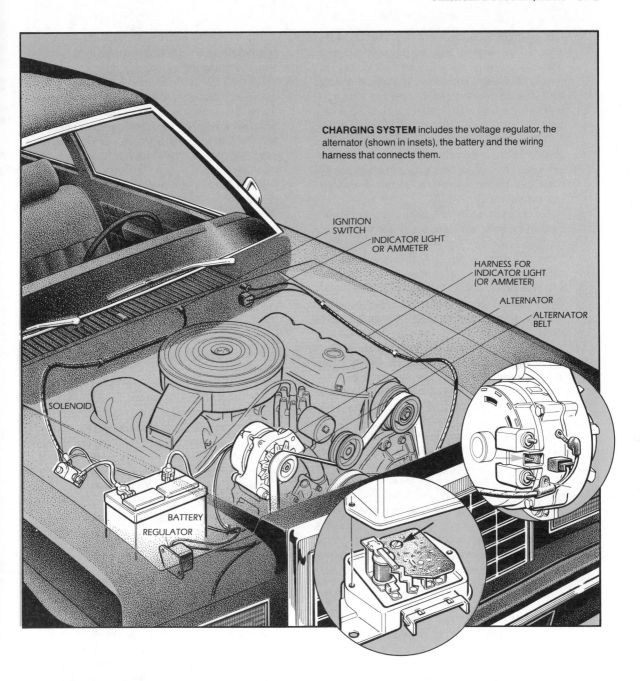

CHARGING SYSTEM includes the voltage regulator, the alternator (shown in insets), the battery and the wiring harness that connects them.

IGNITION SWITCH

INDICATOR LIGHT OR AMMETER

HARNESS FOR INDICATOR LIGHT (OR AMMETER)

ALTERNATOR

ALTERNATOR BELT

SOLENOID

BATTERY

REGULATOR

Charging system troubleshooting

■ MAINTAINING, troubleshooting and repairing the units responsible for producing and controlling electricity in your car isn't such a big deal. Those units are the alternator, voltage regulator and the wiring that connects them to each other and to the units they serve.

As a team, they are called the charging system. The alternator is referred to by some as the a.c. (alternating current) generator and by GM as the Delcotron generator.

Maintenance is a breeze; there's practically none.

General troubleshooting is easy, too, because a glance at the warning light or gauge on the dashboard will usually tell you when the system isn't putting out enough juice. Even if the light or gauge isn't working, the battery will serve as a warning. It will soon discharge (go dead) if the charging system fails.

However, one condition you have to be cautious about is failure of the voltage regulator to limit alternator output. Without regulation, an alternator will overcharge the battery, which can ruin components that use electricity.

For instance, bulbs and fuses that can't handle excessive current will burn out. Battery electrolyte (sulfuric acid) will vaporize quickly if too much charging current is supplied. Unless you spot the depleting electrolyte supply soon enough, dry plates will deteriorate, and the battery will die. An overcharged battery can even explode.

In this respect, you're better off with a conventional battery, especially if you're in the habit of removing vent caps and checking electrolyte level once every week or two. If the electrolyte is frequently found to be low, the system is probably overcharging. Even if you don't check electrolyte level you may get whiffs of the gas. It smells like rotten eggs.

A sealed maintenance-free battery offers no latitude. The first sign that overcharging is destroying the battery is when the battery indicator turns pale yellow or clear, but by then it's too late. However, if your car is equipped with a voltmeter or ammeter, you can easily spot an overcharging condition. If battery voltage frequently exceeds 14.5 volts, or if an ammeter shows continuous high charge rates, overcharging is likely and a basic charging system diagnostic test should be performed.

No task too tough—

Specific troubleshooting procedures that determine if a fault lies with the alternator, regulator or wiring is a bit more difficult than maintenance and general troubleshooting, but it's not as tough as some people would have you believe.

Only when you uncover a fault inside the alternator does the situation become hairy, but even then you have a choice. You can replace the alternator, which is easy but expensive. Or you can tear it down, test internal components and try making repairs to save yourself some money. Advanced Saturday mechanics certainly have the capability to do these things on some cars. Even Saturday mechanics with limited experience may want to try it. There's nothing to lose.

The only maintenance needed is to check the drive belt, which is something you probably do anyway when servicing the cooling system.

Look for cracks on the underside of the belt, since a cracked belt can break without warning. Also look for oil, grease and hard glaze on the underside of the belt, which will cause a belt to slip on its pulleys. A belt that fails to grip pulleys can't turn the alternator rotor fast enough. The result is a reduction in electrical output.

A belt that has stretched and lost tension may also be the reason why your warning light or gauge is showing reduced current output. Make a quick test by pressing down on the belt with your thumb midway between two pulleys. If the belt deflects more than ½ inch or so, that belt is too loose.

Adjusting belt tension

To remove or adjust an alternator drive belt in most vehicles, loosen the pivot and adjusting arm bolts. If you want to slacken the belt so you can remove it, push the alternator toward the engine. When the belt goes limp, pry it off its pulleys. Then, roll a new belt back on the pulleys. *Caution:* Be sure to get a belt of the correct size for your vehicle.

To adjust belt tension, hold a pry bar against the solid part of the alternator housing and pull the alternator away from the engine until the belt tightens. Pick a solid point. Do not pry against the cooling fins or fan, or you'll damage the alternator.

What's proper tension? That depends on whether you're using the finger method or a belt tension gauge to make the judgment. For accuracy, use a gauge. The most common type has a tang that slides under the belt and two arms that fit on top.

Vehicle manufacturers provide "new" and "old" belt tension specifications in service manuals. Instructions that accompany gauges also give some. Remember: A belt is no longer "new" after it's been used for 10 minutes.

If you don't have a gauge, press down on the belt and continue pulling back on the alternator until the belt deflects about ¼ to ½ inch in the center of the belt's longest span. Then, tighten the adjusting arm bolt and the pivot bolt in that order. Do not tighten a belt so much that it gives less than ¼ inch. A too-tight belt can damage alternator bearings.

Some alternators are equipped with a jackscrew belt tensioner. This is simply a screw that is threaded through part of the alternator bracket. When the screw is turned clockwise, the alternator is forced away from the engine and belt tension is increased.

Some Ford V8s from '79 onward and the '84 Corvette use a single serpentine belt to drive all engine

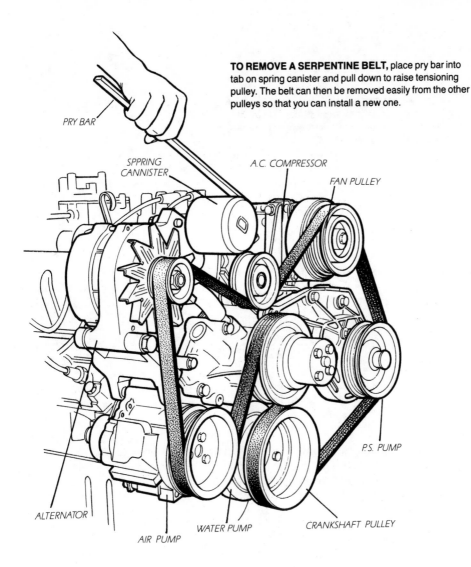

TO REMOVE A SERPENTINE BELT, place pry bar into tab on spring canister and pull down to raise tensioning pulley. The belt can then be removed easily from the other pulleys so that you can install a new one.

PRY BAR

SPPRING CANNISTER

A.C. COMPRESSOR

FAN PULLEY

P.S. PUMP

ALTERNATOR

AIR PUMP

WATER PUMP

CRANKSHAFT PULLEY

accessories. It has a spring-loaded tensioner, so it never needs tightening. But it should be checked and replaced if it is cracked, glazed, oil-soaked or frayed on either side (both sides of the belt drive various pulleys).

Squeal is a common sound produced by a slick drive belt or one that possesses minor surface irregularities. An alternator that is developing a bearing problem can also squeal. How can you tell if the squeal is coming from the belt, alternator or somewhere else in the engine compartment? Apply aerosol belt dressing to the belt. If the squeal is no longer present or changes pitch, you have a noisy belt. If the noise stays the same, the trouble may be inside the alternator. Remove the belt and run the engine. If the problem is in the alternator, the noise will disappear.

Test the battery first

When something happens that suggests a charging system problem, you can't overlook the battery.

The battery, alternator and voltage regulator are closely intertwined. When a problem arises that affects one, it affects all. Watch for the following trouble signs:

■ If the vehicle has a warning light and it stays lighted with the engine idling or until engine speed is increased to about 2,000 rpm, the system should be tested. If the warning light doesn't come on when the ignition switch is turned on (engine not running), forget the charging system and test the light circuit (see section below).

■ If the car has a gauge and it shows discharge with the engine running at a speed just above idle,

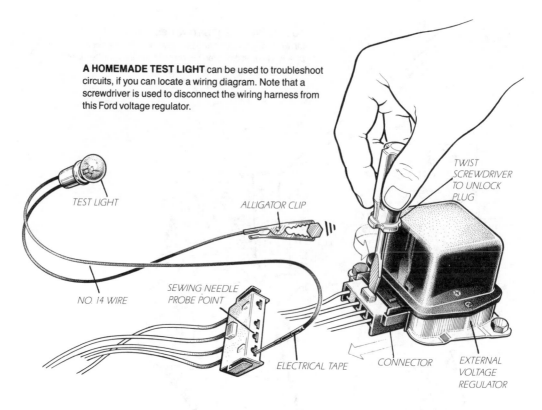

A HOMEMADE TEST LIGHT can be used to troubleshoot circuits, if you can locate a wiring diagram. Note that a screwdriver is used to disconnect the wiring harness from this Ford voltage regulator.

TEST LIGHT

ALLIGATOR CLIP

TWIST SCREWDRIVER TO UNLOCK PLUG

NO. 14 WIRE

SEWING NEEDLE PROBE POINT

ELECTRICAL TAPE

CONNECTOR

EXTERNAL VOLTAGE REGULATOR

the system should be tested. If the gauge shows neither charge nor discharge with the engine running, test the gauge circuit before turning your attention to the battery and charging system (see section below).

■ If the battery has to be charged or refilled with water often, the system should be tested.

■ If headlights dim excessively with the engine running at idle (but brighten when accelerating), the charging system should be tested.

■ If the engine cranks sluggishly, the system should be tested.

■ If you suspect overcharging, the system should be tested.

■ If the battery discharges completely and the vehicle fails to start, the system should be tested.

The first part of any charging system test is battery inspection and diagnosis. Once you've determined that the battery is okay, you can proceed to other tests. But first, let's backtrack and discuss what you should do if your warning light fails to glow when you first turn the key or if your gauge needle stays dead center, showing neither charge nor discharge with the engine running.

Checking the warning light

If a warning light fails, the bulb may be shot or

there may be an open circuit. You can find out by fabricating a warning lamp test light, using a socket that accepts a No. 97 bulb, two lengths of No. 14 wire, an alligator clip and a probe such as a sewing needle. The drawing on the previous page, lower left, shows how to assemble these parts.

With the ignition switch off, connect the test light alligator clip to a clean metal part, such as a bolt. Then, place the test light probe in contact with the wire terminal on the warning light.

Turn the ignition switch on (do not crank the engine).

If the test light glows, but the warning light doesn't, the warning light bulb is burned out or the bulb socket is defective.

If neither the test light nor warning light glows, there is a problem in the warning light circuit.

Testing the warning light in a GM vehicle with an internally mounted voltage regulator (VR) is done differently. Let's use the Delcotron as an example, since the vast majority of internal VRs are found on GM cars. You don't need to use a test light—only your eyes and hands.

If the warning light glows with the ignition switch off, disconnect the two leads from terminals 1 and 2 on the back end of the Delcotron. If the warning light stays on, there's a short in the circuit between the two leads. If the warning light goes out, the rectifier bridge inside the alternator is defective, so replace it. If your battery has been losing charge, the rectifier bridge could be the source of the problem.

If the warning light does *not* go on when you turn the ignition switch on without cranking the engine, the warning light fuse has blown, the warning light bulb or socket is defective, or there's an open circuit in the No. 1 wire between the regulator and light. This condition can also be caused by a faulty rectifier bridge.

Finally, if the warning light stays on with the engine running, there's most likely trouble with the alternator or regulator.

If a gauge needle doesn't move off dead center, you don't have to go through this fuss. With the

ignition switch off, turn on the headlights. If the needle deflects toward *discharge,* the gauge is working. If the needle doesn't move, there's a loose connection at the gauge, an open circuit in the gauge wiring, or the gauge itself is on the fritz.

Troubleshooting alternators

When it comes to testing an alternator and regulator, someone may ask, ''Don't we have to use an adjustable carbon pile (rheostat) and ammeter?''

No, you don't have to. However, you can't be absolutely certain that a charging system is capable of delivering full current without doing a carbon pile load test.

But a basic test of charging system effectiveness can be performed with a voltmeter. The voltmeter

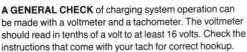

A GENERAL CHECK of charging system operation can be made with a voltmeter and a tachometer. The voltmeter should read in tenths of a volt to at least 16 volts. Check the instructions that come with your tach for correct hookup.

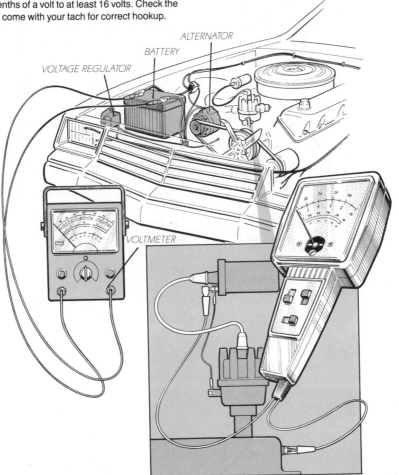

should read in tenths of a volt and be capable of measuring at least 16 volts.

While this test can't actually measure alternator effectiveness under all conditions, it can determine if the battery is being charged by the system. It can also tell you what part of the charging system is at fault if the battery is not being charged.

To test a charging system that has an *externally* mounted regulator, warm up the engine to avoid the possibility of a cold regulator giving false test results. Then, turn off the engine and all electrical accessories and lights. Connect an engine tachometer, following the instructions that come with the tach. Then, attach the voltmeter's positive lead to the battery's positive post and the voltmeter's negative lead to the battery's negative post.

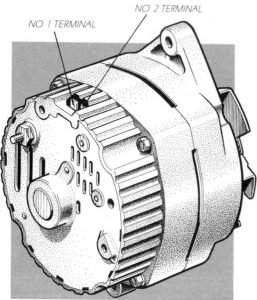

NO. 1 TERMINAL

NO. 2 TERMINAL

TO CHECK WARNING LIGHT of a GM charging system with an internal regulator alternator, remove wires from terminals 1 and 2.

Make a note of the voltmeter (battery voltage) reading. It should be no less than 12 volts. If it is less, the battery is undercharged, so charge the battery. Take another reading and record this battery *base voltage.*

Now, start the engine and slowly increase speed until the tachometer records 1,500 rpm. This is called the *no-load test.* When the voltmeter needle stabilizes, read the meter. You'll get one of two indications:

1. If the voltage reading exceeds the base voltage by 2.0 volts or less, skip down this page to the load test.

2. If the voltage reading exceeds the base voltage by *more* than 2.0 volts, you're faced with a faulty regulator, a bad regulator ground or a short circuit in the wiring harness between the regulator and alternator.

Remove, clean, reinstall and tighten the regulator attaching bolts. Also, clean off the surface on which the regulator sits to assure a good ground.

Do the no-load test again. If you now get a reading that exceeds the base voltage reading by *more* than 2.0 volts, either the regulator is defective or there is a short in the wiring harness. Check the harness for abuse. If you don't detect any, try replacing the regulator.

Note: When mounting a new regulator, see that the mounting surface is clean, bolts are as tight as possible and the ground wire from the alternator, if there is one, is secured under one of the mounting bolts.

If you find a short in the wiring harness, you may still have to replace both the regulator and the wiring, since the short may have damaged the regulator.

Doing a load test

Turn headlights and all electrical accessories on. Increase engine speed to 3,000 rpm and note the voltmeter reading. One of the following will result:

1. If the voltage exceeds base voltage by 0.5 volts or more, the charging system is at least capable of keeping your battery charged under normal conditions.

2. If the voltage increase is less than 0.5 volt, the regulator, the wiring or the alternator is defective. "Full fielding" the charging system can help you pinpoint the problem.

Do the load test next to find a problem in a charging system having an externally mounted regulator. With the tachometer and voltmeter connected as for the no-load test, start the engine. Turn the heater or air conditioner on and set the blower at high speed.

How to full field a vehicle

To full field a late-model Ford with an externally mounted regulator, turn off the engine, disconnect the regulator connector and connect a jumper wire between the "A" and "F" terminals of the regulator plug.

To full field a late-model Chrysler with an externally mounted regulator, turn off the engine and disconnect the green field wire that connects the regulator to the alternator field terminal at the alternator. Then connect a jumper wire from the alternator field terminal to ground.

With either system full-fielded, repeat the load test. If voltage exceeds base voltage by 0.5 or more volts, the regulator is defective and must be replaced. If the increase is less than 0.5 volts, the problem is in the wiring or alternator. There are tests that can help determine which, but they vary a great deal from vehicle to vehicle. However, the alternator is usually the source of the problem. If a visual check of the wiring harness for the alternator/regulator doesn't show signs of abuse or heat, you can be reasonably certain that the alternator is the source of your difficulty.

If the alternator is defective, it will have to be removed from the vehicle for further testing and repair.

Caution: In doing the tests we've just discussed on a vehicle that has a catalytic converter, try to wrap things up within a total engine running time of five minutes. If you exceed this, there's a possibility you'll damage the converter. If you must go beyond five minutes, turn off the engine for 30 minutes so the catalyst can cool down before you continue testing.

TO DO A FULL FIELD TEST on a Ford with an external regulator, disconnect the regulator wiring plug and connect a jumper wire between the A and the F terminals of wiring plug.

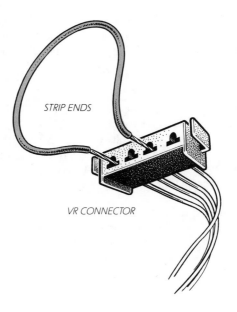

STRIP ENDS

VR CONNECTOR

Underhood cables and wiring

■ ONE OF THE DEMANDS made by battery cables and primary wiring, in particular, is that their connections be clean and tight. If connections aren't clean and tight, resistance to current flow will be high, and hard starting and stalling are likely to result.

Cause of sudden stalls

Primary wiring has been the cause of one of the most baffling failures experienced by car owners. Suppose you are rolling blissfully down the road when—pfft—just like that, the engine stalls. You brake to a halt, turn off the ignition key, scratch your head, turn on the key and crank the engine.

It starts, and the problem doesn't occur again until some later time. What may be causing it?

A loose primary connection could be the reason. Or maybe primary wire insulation has worn down and bare wire is shorting against the distributor housing.

Primary wiring must be kept in good condition. If it shorts out, there will be no voltage, no ignition and no go. Would you think to look inside the distributor for a bare wire?

Sparkplug cables

Obviously, sparkplug cables extend from the distributor cap to the sparkplugs. However, included in this designation is the single high-tension cable that runs from the tower of the ignition coil to the center tower of the distributor cap. Don't forget about it. When it fails, your engine won't start.

Cables don't last forever. They wear out as they get older because they are exposed to high underhood temperature, oil splash and moisture. These cause insulation to become brittle and crack, which gives electricity an area of least resistance to penetrate. Electricity will arc through cracks in the insulation and, accordingly, will be diverted from the sparkplugs.

Reduced current leads to a decrease in combustion efficiency and an increase in fuel consumption. When a sparkplug fails to ignite the fuel mixture, fuel in the affected cylinder is thrown out the exhaust. It is wasted. This is what's known as misfire.

Environment isn't the only factor leading to cable failure. Mechanics employing bad work habits are another. Cables should not be tugged on when they are being disconnected. Strain causes conductive strands to separate, which leads to excessive resistance to current flow. Again, this will result in engine misfire.

Handling cables properly

To handle cables properly, use a pair of sparkplug cable pliers. The tool costs a few dollars, but is worth the money. It helps prevent accidents that can cause cable damage.

To remove cables from sparkplugs using these pliers, grasp the boot covering the plug with the tool, and twist back and forth as you pull the boot from the sparkplug.

If sparkplug cable pliers aren't available, remove cables by firmly grasping the boot and twisting back and forth as you pull. Do not pull the cables. Pull only on the boots!

Testing cables

Look for cracks in insulation. And don't forget the boots. A boot is part of a cable and tends to dry out and crack, too. A bad boot will cause

TREAT your sparkplug cables gently and they won't let you down. Don't pull on the cable; use a special pliers or grasp the boot firmly.

flashover: Electricity will take the path of least resistance and come out through a crack in the boot, sparking across the outside of the sparkplug insulator. Electricity won't get to where it's needed—to the electrode end of the sparkplug.

Current leak

After testing all cables, leave any one sparkplug cable disconnected as you probe the cable and boots between the coil and the center tower of the distributor. One sparkplug cable must remain disconnected while you check the coil-to-distributor cable so that one of the paths of least resistance which the ignition spark would normally follow is removed. Thus if there *is* a current leak in the coil-to-distributor cable it will jump to the screwdriver once during each revolution of the distributor rotor.

Caution: If your car is equipped with a catalytic converter, don't keep sparkplug cables disconnected for any longer than 30 seconds at a time to avoid catalytic converter overheating. Test as many cables as you can in 30 seconds and then test the others after the converter cools down.

If one or more cables are found defective, replace them all. If one bad cable is uncovered, chances are that the others will soon peak out.

When checking sparkplug cables, it is important that you inspect the metal connectors inside the boots on both ends. Corroded or burned connectors will cause excessive resistance. Replace the cables if this damage exists.

Secure cable connections

Important: The main reason for a burned connector (it will be black) is failure to connect cables securely. Keep this in mind whenever you are reconnecting a cable to its sparkplug or seat in the distributor.

After examining cables, test them for excessive resistance to electricity with an ohmmeter that has a scale which reads in thousands of ohms. Lay the cable on a workbench. Turn the ohmmeter on and connect its leads to each end of the cable.

The amount of allowable resistance depends on the length of the cable and may even be marked on the cable. Generally, however, if resistance is greater than 25,000 ohms, discard the cable.

After testing one cable, reinstall it before removing another. This will prevent you from con-

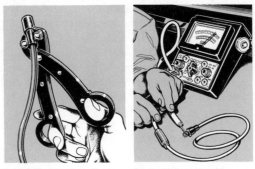

SPARKPLUG pliers (left) are the best way to pull boots. Use an ohmmeter (right) when you measure the resistance of your cables and other wires.

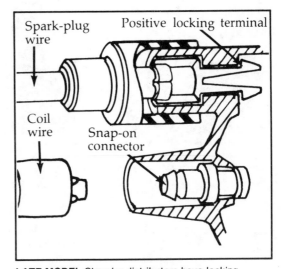

LATE-MODEL Chrysler distributors have locking sparkplug wires that must be removed from inside the cap. Press the hook-spring clips together and push the wire out from inside the cap. The coil wire on these distributor caps snaps into a center-terminal connector.

necting a sparkplug to a wrong tower of the distributor, which will result in out-of-turn plug firing and possible engine damage.

When you reconnect cables, be sure they don't rest against a part that can cut or burn them, such as the throttle linkage or exhaust manifold. See that cables crisscross one another to prevent crossfire.

Crossing up crossfire

Crossfire, which is also called induction leakage, occurs when sparkplug cables are grouped

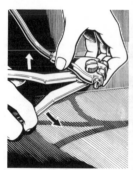

BATTERY TERMINAL spreader (left) is needed to replace terminals easily and without hammering. Side terminal batteries (right) have cables connected as shown.

close together and run parallel. Crossfire causes engine roughness, backfiring and detonation. Engine and sparkplug damage may result.

Crossfire refers to a sparkplug firing out of time because of induction. This means that the strong magnetic electrical field that envelops a sparkplug cable will be absorbed by an adjacent sparkplug to fire out of turn. The condition prevails between two *consecutively* firing cylinders.

The best way to avoid crossfire is to make sure that cables crisscross as they approach sparkplugs so no two physically adjacent cables run parallel. Most automobile manufacturers equip cars with engine-mounted looms that hold cables and help maintain a proper arrangement. If a loom is damaged or lost, replace it.

Battery cables

What you should know about battery cables can be summarized as follows:

1. The cable parts of battery cables don't cause problems nearly as often as the terminal parts of battery cables, especially at battery posts.

2. The best way to prevent trouble from battery-cable terminals is to service them semiannually to prevent corrosion that interferes with electrical flow. Take cables off the battery posts. Useful tools you should consider purchasing if battery posts are on top of your battery are the following:

■ Terminal nut wrench and battery pliers to loosen the terminals' bolts and nuts. Hold the bolt stationary with the wrench and turn the nut with the pliers. Always remove the negative cable first and connect it last, because the path to ground is broken and thus the shock hazard is reduced.

■ A terminal puller whose jaws engage the bottom of the terminal so when the tool's screw is tightened, the terminal is drawn evenly off the battery post.

Caution: Don't bang on the terminal with a hammer to loosen it, and don't try prying it off with a screw driver. That's an excellent way to ruin the battery.

■ A battery cleaning tool to polish terminals and posts. Wash terminals and battery posts with a baking soda solution. Then polish the insides of the terminals with the terminal brush end of the battery cleaning tool. Use the battery post brush end of the cleaning tool to polish posts.

■ A terminal spreader to facilitate putting terminals back on posts. Do not bang the terminals into place with a hammer. You may ruin the battery.

With terminals on battery posts, tighten them securely and spread a light coat of petroleum jelly over them to help retard corrosion.

3. The biggest problem that has been encountered with side battery terminals has been improper torquing, which causes high resistance and hard starting. To service side terminals properly, do the following:

■ Unscrew the negative battery cable.

■ Clean the threads and end of the cable screw thoroughly with a wire brush.

■ If necessary, clean the internal threads in the battery case. Use a small wire brush or a ⅜-16 bottoming tap. If you use a bottoming tap, do not tighten it beyond 70-inch-pounds.

■ Service the positive cable next.

■ Install the positive cable and tighten it to 70-inch-pounds. Then install the negative cable.

4. You should replace a battery cable when insulation wears or cracks, or wires become exposed around terminals. Note the size of the cable you are buying to make sure it's the same size as the old cable.

Alternator checks

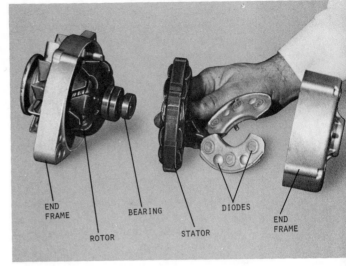

END FRAME · ROTOR · BEARING · STATOR · DIODES · END FRAME

CHECKING INDIVIDUAL alternator components lets you limit replacement costs to those that are bad.

■ ALTERNATORS HAVE been used in U.S.-built cars since the early 1960s. They're also called alternating current (a.c.) generators, or—more loosely—just generators. An older model U.S. car or an import may have a direct current (d.c.) generator instead. You should check. They're quite different breeds, and the information here doesn't apply to d.c. generators.

For decades, all cars had the d.c. version. But more and more electrical accessories—air conditioners, higher-capacity batteries, additional lights, AM-FM radios and tape decks, for example—strained d.c. generators' capacity. Alternators have greater output and weigh less.

The alternator is one of the most reliable, efficient assemblies in a car. So reliable, in fact, that a problem in the electrical system probably comes not from the alternator itself, but some part associated with it.

Chart your solution

The troubleshooting chart lists electrical problems and matches them to causes *not* part of the alternator. Before pulling your alternator from the car, follow the "what to do" procedures. The odds are good you'll solve the problem.

The drive belt is an excellent example of an alternator-associated component that causes problems often blamed unfairly on the alternator itself. In fact, in seven cases of electrical failure of every 10, that belt is the troublemaker.

A drive belt that is loose or worn or slips be-

cause it has become glazed costs you alternator output. Replace a glazed belt. Also replace a damaged belt with a new belt of proper size, properly adjusted. To adjust tension, a belt tension gauge is far more accurate than the "press-by-finger" method. It minimizes overtightening risk that can strain, maybe destroy, bearings.

Tighten a drive belt by using a pry bar against the stator support—never on the end frames. Hold the alternator against its belt and tighten the bracket nuts.

An alternator's components

All alternators consist of a rotor, a stator, and two end frames, one containing the diodes (rectifiers). They're necessary to convert or "rectify" the a.c. output to direct current, required by a car's electrical components.

Basically, the rotor is a field coil wound on an iron core that's mounted between two iron poles. It revolves inside the stator, mounted between the end frames. The stator consists of wire loops wound into slots of a laminated frame. Two spring-loaded brushes are on slip rings on one end of the rotor shaft. Rings are attached to leads from the field coil and brushes are connected through a voltage regulator to the battery.

With the voltage regulator closed, current passes through one brush, through the slip ring on which it rides, and through the field coil or rotor. Then it goes through the other slip ring and brush and back to the battery through the ground path.

The revolving rotor's moving magnetic field cuts across the stator's windings, inducing alternating current. The diodes let current flow in only one direction, to the battery, so they convert the a.c. to d.c.

Most alternators have six diodes—three negative and three positive—often contained in a heat sink. To replace a bad one, you must replace the heat sink and all its diodes. But in other cases, diodes are pressed individually into the end frame.

Voltage regulator, a partner

The voltage regulator controls the alternator field current and regulates the charging rate in the alternator-battery circuit in response to the battery's state of charge. There must be enough electricity to do the job, but not enough to cause overcharging.

A major difference among alternators is in the location of the regulator. Early systems used electromechanical regulators outside the alternator. Solid-state or electronic regulators, also outside the alternator, were the first modification. The latest step has been the electronic regulator within the alternator body.

Domestic cars use six makes of alternators: Chrysler, Delco (GM), Ford, Leece-Neville, Motorola and Prestolite. Whichever you have, whatever its style, whether you plan tests of the alternator itself or its regulator, the service manual or service instructions are essential. Don't plunge ahead without them. They're available from the manufacturer's technical publications department.

For alternator or regulator tests, you need a tachometer and a voltmeter/ammeter with carbonpile rheostat to control voltage. If bench testing is required, you'll also need an ohmmeter.

On the alternator itself, it's wise to begin with an output test; you leave the unit on the car. Besides, if output is OK, the electrical trouble can't be blamed on the alternator itself.

You hook up test instruments according to the instructions and run the engine at the specified speed—say 1250 rpm. Adjust the carbon-pile rheostat so you get the specified voltage, perhaps 15 volts. The ammeter should now say you're getting electrical output to meet the manufacturer's specs.

Moving quickly

Keep in mind that during the alternator output test, the regulator may be out of the circuit. If so, your system doesn't have its protection. So finish the test as quickly as possible and don't exceed engine speed the manufacturer calls for.

This troubleshooting chart deals with electrical problems that may make you believe that the alternator is malfunctioning. In most cases, what appears to be an alternator-induced problem is traceable to some other component. Alternators are seldom to blame for electrical malfunctions in a vehicle.

PROBLEM	CAUSE	WHAT TO DO
Battery low in charge headlights dim at idle. (Note: recurrent unexplainable discharge of the battery suggests need for testing the entire charging system.)	1. Drive belt. 2. Battery cables or electric system wiring. 3. Drain on battery. 4. Battery is damaged or worn out.	1. Adjust or replace. 2. Clean battery cables and terminals. Clean and tighten all wiring connections. 3. Check for drain with ignition "OFF." 4. Test battery capacity. Replace battery if necessary.

PROBLEM	CAUSE	WHAT TO DO
Ammeter registers constant discharge or charging system light remains on; battery doesn't hold charge; low alternator output.	1. Drive belt. 2. Battery cables or electric system wiring.	1. Adjust or replace. 2. Clean battery cables and terminals. Clean and tighten all wiring connections.

PROBLEM	CAUSE	WHAT TO DO
Lights and fuses fail prematurely; short battery life; battery uses excessive water; resistor wire burns; coil damage; high charging rate.	1. Electric system wiring. 2. Regulator.	1. Clean and tighten all wiring. Replace damaged wires. 2. Replace a bad regulator.

PROBLEM	CAUSE	WHAT TO DO
Noise.	1. Drive belt. 2. Water pump.	1. Treat or replace a squealing belt. 2. Check the water pump with a sound detecting tool, such as a stethoscope, to assure that it's not to blame rather than the alternator.

Drive belt checks

■ DON'T IGNORE drive belts until they snap—it makes a lot more sense to give them some reasonable maintenance. A belt failure on the road can mean loss of engine cooling, charging, power steering, air-conditioning and loss of your temper if you don't have spares.

Thorough inspection

Whenever you do underhood service, take a few minutes to inspect each drive belt. Twist each belt over and look for all of the following; any one is cause for replacement:

■ **Cracks in the underside** (the surface that rides flat against the surface between the pulley rims). Cracks create hinge points that allow excessive flexing. The belt can split apart at any crack.

■ **Peeling from the underside.** This results in a rough surface, and the belt will transfer power unevenly. Belt failure will be sudden.

■ **Split in the sidewall.** A drive belt is something like a tire in that there is a supporting layer of cord between the rubberized surfaces. If there is a separation in the sidewall, often at the cord layer, the belt will not ride the pulleys properly and may fail at any instant.

■ **Glaze on the sides or underside of the belt.** A slick, hard glazing on the sides or underside of the belt is caused by belt slippage. The accessories are not driven properly, resulting in a low battery, engine overheating, poor air conditioning performance and erratic power steering. The slipping belt itself overheats and will fail.

■ **Oil-soaked belt.** A belt that is oil-soaked has been softened and will come apart. Because all belt dressings contain some oil-base penetrant that ultimately softens the belt, they are no solution to belt squeal, even if they temporarily eliminate this noise, which is normally caused by looseness.

Thumb pressure on a belt, midway between pulleys, has been the traditional way to check belt tension. On older cars, up to a half-inch deflection under the pressure has been standard "rule of thumb" for an adequately tightened belt. On today's cars, however, this is not acceptable for these reasons: 1. There is a substantial variation in the deflections under the thumbs of any two people. 2. Accessibility is such that you could never measure the deflection accurately even if you have a calibrated thumb. 3. Deflection is not a positive indicator of tension.

The belt-tension gauge is the simplest way to test tension accurately. It hooks over the belt and when released provides a number—pounds of tension—to compare with specifications developed by the carmaker. The belt can be adjusted to specs in a single operation on most cars.

Adjusting tension

Most drive belts are adjusted by loosening mounting bolts for the accessory or loosening an idler pulley (belt guide), then applying tension on the component with a pry bar, and tightening the adjusting bolt.

There are some exceptions. The simplest is an access hole in the adjusting bracket, so that the pry bar is positioned precisely, and not against something delicate, such as the air-cooling fins of an alternator.

A square hole in the accessory, or idler pulley that accepts a ½-inch drive breaker bar is another popular design. Again, the object is to make sure you don't pry against a part that can't take the strain.

A cam-type adjuster on an idler pulley is used on the Dodge Colt. You slacken the retaining nut, put a wrench on a partial hex section of the pulley and turn (one way to loosen the belt, the other way to tighten). When tension is correct, you tighten the retaining nut.

A stud-nut adjuster used on Ford power steer-

HOW TO TAKE CARE OF YOUR CAR'S DRIVE BELTS

BELT TENSION is best checked using the type of gauge shown here.

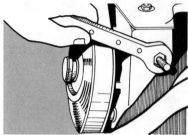

STUDNUT ADJUSTER on power steering pump is tensioning device on Fords.

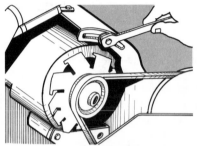

BRACKET with slot is most common means of belt-tension adjustment.

PULLEY NUT is loosened on VW while screwdriver is wedged to hold pulley.

PULLEY HALVES are separated to remove belt on ageless Beetle.

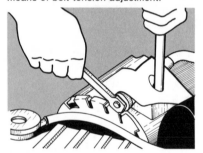

PILOT HOLE for pry bar, as used on Chevette, is accurate and convenient.

ADJUSTER is turned to tension idler pulley on the Dodge Colt.

ing pumps eliminates the need to apply tension with any kind of bar. The pump is mounted on a bracket with studs through elongated bracket holes and retaining nuts. You slacken the retaining nuts, then turn a separate stud-nut adjuster. This moves the stud in or out, repositioning the pump along the elongated holes in the mounting bracket. When tension is correct, tighten the retaining nuts and you're done.

The Volkswagen Beetle, a car that seems to live forever, is an exception to just about all rules regarding drive belts. On the VW, you can check tension with your thumb, and the belt is so wide open, you can even get a ruler into position to measure the deflection (10 mm or ⅜ inch is the spec).

The adjustment is with shims on a generator/fan pulley that comes apart. You wedge a screwdriver through a slot in the inner pulley half

and against the engine to hold the pulley, then remove the nut holding the halves together. To increase tension, you remove some shims from between the pulley halves so the halves will come closer together when tightened, forcing the belt to ride higher between rims of the pulley halves. To reduce tension, add shims, which are stored between the outer pulley half and nut. It's a pure cut-and-dried operation.

When a new belt is called for, double-check others for possible replacement, particularly if you're changing an outer belt.

Push the idler pulley or accessory all the way in (in the case of the stud-nut adjuster, back it all the way out), and the new belt should just fit onto the pulleys. You may have to pry a new belt over a pulley rim with a screwdriver, but a new belt should never fit so easily that you are near the outer limits of proper tension adjustment.

Chest in the Spanish style

■ THIS HANDSOME SPANISH chest is as easy to build as it is to look at. The dark stained wood and mosaic-tile top will add richness to any room.

To determine the dimensions of your chest, first select your tile. Then, alter top dimensions to fit the tile chosen to avoid extra cutting.

On the chest shown, we used an imported mosaic tile which came in 1-ft. squares on paper backing. After laying squares on the plywood top, add ½ in. (in width and length) to the plywood to give you a ¼-in. grout line around the perimeter. Ceramic tiles come in 4¼, 6 and 12-in. sizes, with thickness ranging from ¼ to ¾ in.

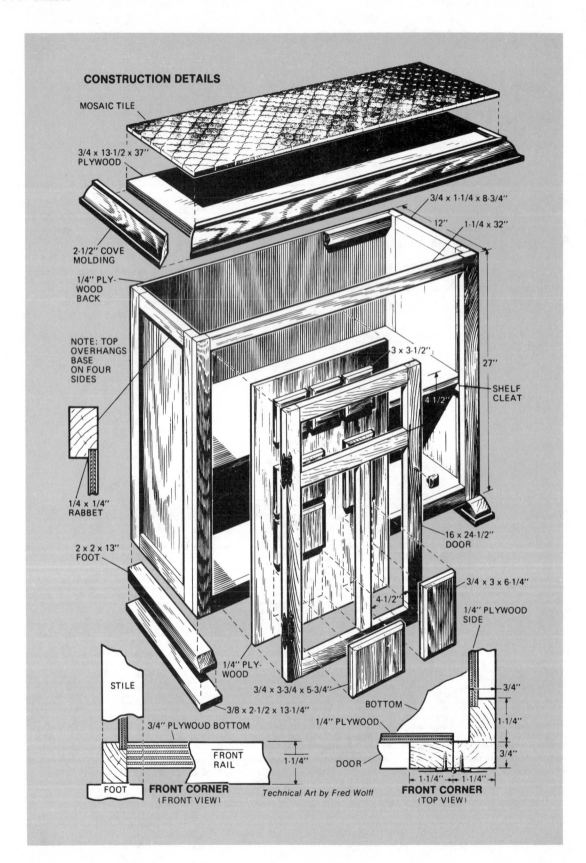

CONSTRUCTION DETAILS

MOSAIC TILE

3/4 x 13-1/2 x 37" PLYWOOD

3/4 x 1-1/4 x 8-3/4"

12"   1-1/4 x 32"

2-1/2" COVE MOLDING

1/4" PLY-WOOD BACK

3 x 3-1/2"

27"

NOTE: TOP OVERHANGS BASE ON FOUR SIDES

4 1/2"

SHELF CLEAT

1/4 x 1/4" RABBET

16 x 24-1/2" DOOR

2 x 2 x 13" FOOT

3/4 x 3 x 6-1/4"

1/4" PLYWOOD SIDE

4-1/2"

1/4" PLY-WOOD

STILE

3/4 x 3-3/4 x 5-3/4"

3/4"

BOTTOM

1-1/4"

3/8 x 2-1/2 x 13-1/4"

1/4" PLYWOOD

3/4"

3/4" PLYWOOD BOTTOM

FRONT RAIL

1-1/4"

DOOR

FOOT   **FRONT CORNER**
(FRONT VIEW)

Technical Art by Fred Wolff

1-1/4"   1-1/4"

FRONT CORNER
(TOP VIEW)

The 12 x 27-in. end panels were made with 1¼-in. framing (stiles and rails) ripped from ¾-in. stock and rabbeted. Then ¼-in. plywood was glued in the rabbets. Though the drawing shows the plywood let into edge-rabbets, it could be simply glued and tacked to the inside of the framing.

The doors were framed with ¾ x 1¼-in. stock and the ¼-in. plywood backup panel was glued and nailed to the frames with short brads.

Panel blocks were cut from ¾-in. stock and fastened to the plywood backing with small brads and white glue. For a sculptured look, bevel the blocks along the top edges with the table saw set at 45°. When you lay out the blocks, leave at least ⅝ in. around each block.

The feet were ripped 1½ in. wide from 2 x 4 stock and then beveled 45° at the front. These, in turn, were glued to the lower feet and the leg setup was then fastened to the cabinet with flathead screws.

Edge (cove) molding is fastened to the plywood top so that it sits above the plywood the thickness of the tile and mastic. With the molding placed before the tile, the former can then serve as a leveling guide when you lay the tile. Apply the mastic with a notched trowel and let it set about 15 minutes.

As you position each tile tap it lightly with a hammer and clean wood block to assure a tight bond.

Next day mix dry grout and water to the consistency of mayonnaise. Apply grout between tiles with a straightedge to rake it into the spaces. The grout should dry in about 30 minutes.

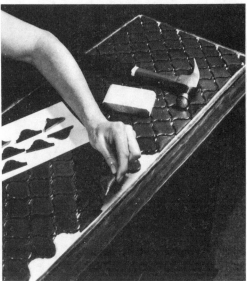

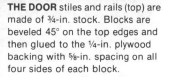

THE DOOR stiles and rails (top) are made of ¾-in. stock. Blocks are beveled 45° on the top edges and then glued to the ¼-in. plywood backing with ⅝-in. spacing on all four sides of each block.

THE PLYWOOD-TOP size is determined by the tile you use. In the case above, 1-ft. square mosaic tile was applied using mastic. Half tiles are used around the perimeter to complete the surface.

THE TILE GROUT is raked diagonally between tiles with straightedge (left). After a wait of about 30 minutes the excess grout should be washed off the surface of the tile with a sponge and water.

Period pieces from stock moldings

■ THERE ARE PROBABLY several good reasons Spanish or Mediterranean-style furniture enjoys the designer and decorator status it does today. The massive, sculpted look of the deeply carved, recessed panels blends well with practically all decor. The rugged-looking finish can take the abuse that it's certain to receive in a home with youngsters. Minor nicks or dents in the finish are practically invisible and, in fact,

BARGAIN-PRICE cedar chest before moldings were applied. It was bought at a thrift shop for $2.

can add charm to the piece. Your youngsters can sometimes be your own antiquing specialists.

It's not necessary to be a woodcarver or woodworking artisan to duplicate the look. Using stock moldings available at any lumberyard, you can achieve the effect with simple butted joints. Take a trip to your nearby lumberyard and look at some of the stock moldings. The different moldings you find may give you original ideas for your own purposes. Or you can make original moldings using your shaper or router. Though this is more work, it may give you just the look you are trying to achieve.

The cedar chest shown here was purchased in a junk shop for a couple of dollars. It was battered, its veneer was half peeled off and it was shabby looking. No doubt you can also find one in a secondhand store, junk shop or even in your attic.

To finish this old chest, the veneer was reglued, the old ball-type feet removed and the piece was sanded down to bare wood. Sometimes an old chest can have many coats of paint or varnish as

MOLDINGS AT CORNERS are miter-joined; horizontals and verticals inside have 45° bevel undercut.

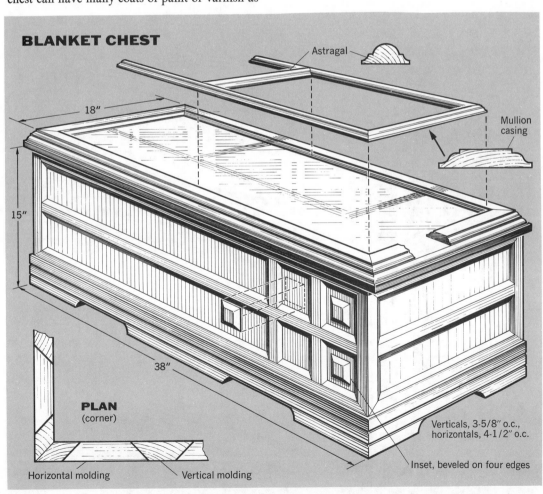

BLANKET CHEST

Astragal

Mullion casing

18″

15″

38″

PLAN (corner)

Horizontal molding   Vertical molding

Verticals, 3-5/8″ o.c., horizontals, 4-1/2″ o.c.

Inset, beveled on four edges

VARIATION ON AN old chest. In the original state, it had beveled drawer fronts and plain, flat doors.

well as dirt on it, so be sure you get down to the bare wood when sanding. Once you decide on the moldings to use, make a scale drawing of the piece to determine the on-center locations for vertical and horizontal pieces. With this calculated, all you have to do is cut the required number of pieces.

Use miter cuts at the outside corner joints. On the inside strips of molding, simply make straight crosscuts with a 45° bevel and butt the pieces. But if the molding you select has a sharp edge, perpendicular joints will have to be made with either 45° saw cuts or by coping. Apply the molding to the outside corners first, then add the interior pieces. If you plan to paint and antique the chest, you can use white glue and brads to assemble it. The brads eliminate the need for clamping.

A final touch, a matter of personal choice, is to add the small, beveled blocks of the same molding to each recessed square. Depending on the piece, this will often add a bit of extra charm.

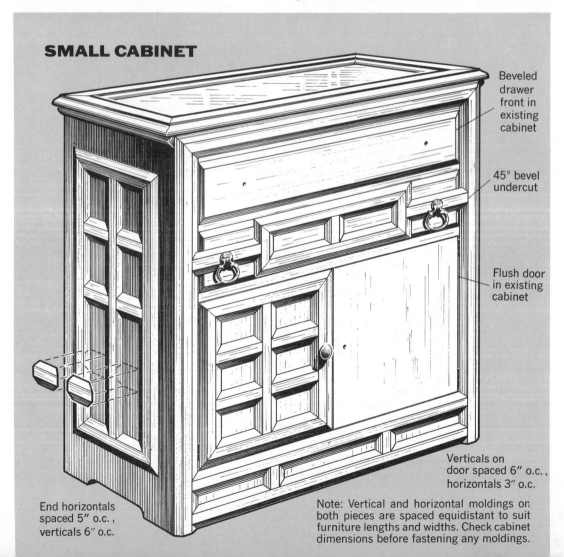

SMALL CABINET

Beveled drawer front in existing cabinet

45° bevel undercut

Flush door in existing cabinet

End horizontals spaced 5″ o.c., verticals 6″ o.c.

Verticals on door spaced 6″ o.c., horizontals 3″ o.c.

Note: Vertical and horizontal moldings on both pieces are spaced equidistant to suit furniture lengths and widths. Check cabinet dimensions before fastening any moldings.

Pop-top desk

■ HERE'S A SURE WAY to involve youngsters from 3 to 10 in crafts and hobbies. This pop-top desk boasts a tilting top that can be positioned to suit the activity at hand—from flat for jigsaw puzzles and games to a steep pitch for working on paintings. The plans to build the chair are an added bonus.

Though the original desk is sized to suit ages 3 to 10, you can increase the dimensions proportionately to meet the needs of teen-agers or adults, if desired. All will delight in using this functional piece with its storage for supplies used in crafts and hobbies.

Pop-top desk features

A neat swing-out tray on the left provides easy access to small items that must be kept handy. Two roomy drawers and the storage compartments under the tilting tabletop will hold a fair amount of art supplies, games and other items. The compartment under the hinged seat adds even more storage space.

A roll of 18-in.-wide sketching paper or newsprint conveniently feeds out of a slot in the front apron. It should be noted that 18-in.-wide sketching paper in rolls is commonly available at

art supply stores. Newsprint is usually sold in 36-in.-wide rolls. If you opt for the less expensive newsprint, you can buy the wide roll and cut it in half on your band saw.

The prime consideration in designing the desk was making sure the tilting top was safe. Folding metal brackets and adjustable lid supports that require forceful tightening were ruled out because of the possibility of accidental slipping, which could crush a tiny finger or hand. The novel and positive-holding four-position, tilting-top supports contrived for this table do the job nicely and safely.

The top is elevated by lifting it at back center with one hand until the desired notches in the supports flop into place. The crossbar between the supports facilitates lowering the top: One hand can pull out on the bar to disengage the supports, while the other hand holds and lowers the top.

Another safety feature is found in the drawers: They can't be pulled out of their compartments accidentally. The drawer stops have two 1½-in. common nails with the points blunted. They're dropped through holes above each drawer. The drawer backs strike these projecting nails and effectively stop when contact is made.

Building the desk

Common No. 2 grade pine carefully selected for small tight knots and ½-in. MDO plywood as well as ¼-in. lauan plywood are used for this project.

MDO is Medium Density Overlaid fir plywood. It has a tough, smooth, resin-coated surface that can be cut without splintering; it is especially well suited for painting. This material also has better-quality inner plies so you won't have the usual problem of large voids, common in ordinary fir plywood. It's a bit more expensive, but well worth the difference. Be sure to order S/2/S—surfaced two sides.

Cut 1 x 6 boards to size for the front and side aprons, then cut ¼ x ⅜-in. rabbets on the inside bottoms. Lay out the rectangle for the swing-out tray opening on the left side apron. Bore corner holes, then use the table saw to make two parallel cuts in line with the holes.

To do this, depress the blade, set the fence and position the work. Hold down the work with one hand, turn on the power and slowly elevate the blade until it cuts through the top surface. Advance the piece as required. Use a sabre saw or jigsaw to make the end cuts to drop out the waste. Next, cut the slot for the roll paper in the front apron, following the same table-saw technique.

Use the router with a V-cutter to bevel the edges of the slot on both sides. A block of wood clamped to the router base as shown will guide it properly.

DESK
MATERIALS LIST

Key	No.	Size and description (use)
		TABLE
A	4	¾ x 3½ x 23½" pine (leg)
B	2	¾ x 4¼ x 32½" pine (apron)
C	2	¾ x 4¼ x 19½" pine (apron)
D	1	¾ x 4 x 19½" pine (partition)
E	2	¾ x 2 x 21" pine (stretcher)
F	1	¾ x 2 x 31" pine (stretcher)
G	1	½ x 7 x 34" MDO plywood (shelf)
H	1	¼ x 20¼ x 31¾" lauan plywood (bottom)
I	1	¼ x 3 x 13" lauan plywood (partition)
J	2	½ x ¾ x 3" pine (cleat)
K	1	¾ x 1½ x 13" pine (tray support)
L	2	¾"-dia. x 2½" hardwood dowel (pin)
M	1	¾"-dia. x 22½" hardwood dowel (paper roller)
N	1	⅜"-dia. x 2" hardwood dowel (handle)
		DRAWER CABINET
O	1	½ x 13 x 18½" MDO plywood (top)
P	2	½ x 8 x 18½" MDO plywood (side)
Q	2	½ x 11 x 18" MDO plywood (shelf)
R	1	½ x 8 x 11" MDO plywood (back)
		DRAWERS (2 REQD.)
S	2	¾ x 3 7/16 x 10⅞" pine (front)
T	4	½ x 3 7/16 x 17⅜" MDO plywood (side)
U	2	½ x 3 7/16 x 9⅞" MDO plywood (back)
V	2	¼ x 10⅜ x 16⅜" lauan plywood (bottom)
		TABLETOP
W	1	½ x 24 x 37" MDO plywood (top)
X	2	½ x 4 x 17⅜" MDO plywood (support)
Y	2	½ x 1¼ x 3" MDO plywood (cleat)
Z	4	3" flat corner irons
AA	1	½"-dia. x 35" hardwood dowel (spacer)
BB	1	¾"-dia. half-round x 34" pine (pencil stop)
CC	1	1½" x 30" continuous hinges
		SWING-OUT TRAY
DD	1	¾ x 3 x 13⅞" pine (face)
EE	1	½ x 1¾ x 12⅜" MDO plywood (front)
FF	1	½ x 1¾ x 9⅜" MDO plywood (side)
GG	1	½ x 1¾ x 9⅜" MDO plywood (back)
HH	1	1¾ x 2 x 13" pine, cut from 8/4 or glued-up stock (curved side)
II	1	¼ x 10⅜ x 12⅞" lauan plywood (bottom)
JJ	1	3 x 3 1/16" brass butt hinge
KK	4	⅜"-dia. x 1½" hardwood dowel (hinge dowels)
LL	*	⅜"-dia. wood plugs
MM	*	1¼" No. 8 fh screws
NN	3	2" No. 8 rh screws and washers
OO	2	1½" common nail (drawer stop)
PP	4	¾" No. 8 fh screw
QQ	2	1" x 8-32 fh machine screw and locknut
RR	*	1½" finishing nails
SS	1	Knob, Amerock No. T-726
TT	*	⅞" brads
Misc.:		Carpenter's glue

*As required.

DESIGN INCLUDES a swing-out tray, two drawers and pencil-stop to keep supplies from rolling or sliding off the desk top when tilted.

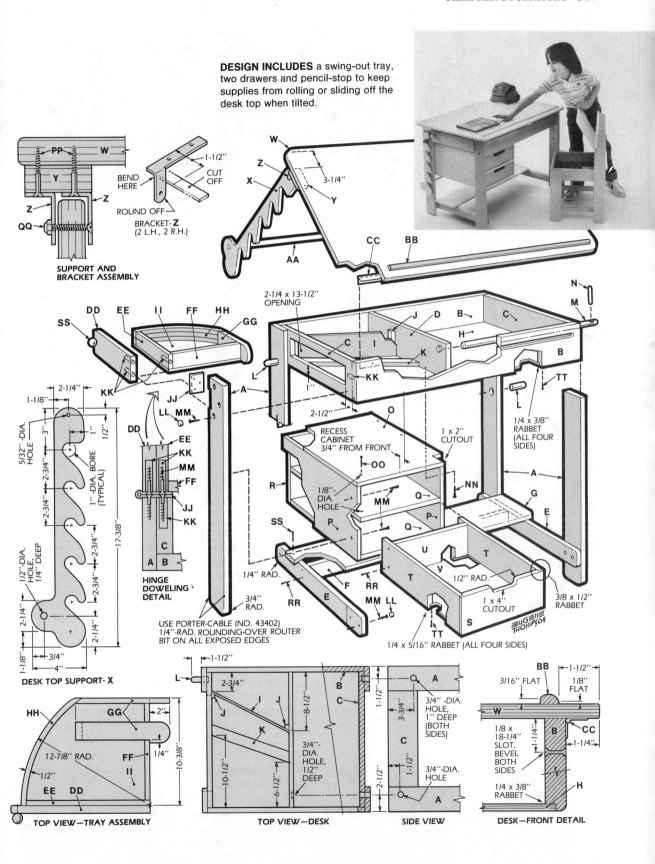

SUPPORT AND BRACKET ASSEMBLY

PP W
Y
Z
Z
QQ

1-1/2"
CUT OFF
BEND HERE
ROUND OFF
BRACKET-**Z**
(2 L.H., 2 R.H.)

W
Z
X
Y
3-1/4"
AA

CC BB

2-1/4 x 13-1/2" OPENING

N
M
J D B C
H
B
TT

1/4 x 3/8" RABBET (ALL FOUR SIDES)

DD EE II FF HH GG
SS

C I
K
KK
L
A
L
2-1/2"
1"

RECESS CABINET 3/4" FROM FRONT
1 x 2" CUTOUT
OO
A
G
E

JJ
LL MM
DD
EE KK MM FF JJ KK
C
A B

HINGE DOWELING DETAIL

R
1/8"-DIA. HOLE
MM
Q
NN
P P
Q
P

SS
1/4" RAD.
RR
E F
RR
MM LL
U V T
T
1/2" RAD.
S
1 x 4" CUTOUT
3/8 x 1/2" RABBET

TT
1/4 x 5/16" RABBET (ALL FOUR SIDES)

USE PORTER-CABLE (NO. 43402) 1/4"-RAD. ROUNDING-OVER ROUTER BIT ON ALL EXPOSED EDGES

3/4" RAD.

DESK TOP SUPPORT- X

2-1/4"
1-1/8"
5/32"-DIA. HOLE
3"
1"
1/2"
2-3/4"
1" DIA. BORE (TYPICAL)
2-3/4"
2-3/4"
17-3/8"
2-3/4"
1/2"-DIA. HOLE, 1/4" DEEP
2-1/4"
2-1/4"
1-1/8"
3/4"
4"

TOP VIEW—TRAY ASSEMBLY
HH
GG
2"
12-7/8" RAD.
FF
1/4"
10-3/8"
II
1/2"
EE DD

TOP VIEW—DESK
L
1-1/2"
2-3/4"
J I J
J
K
8-1/2"
10-1/2"
6-1/2"
3/4"-DIA. HOLE, 1/2" DEEP
B
C

SIDE VIEW
A
1-1/2"
3-3/4"
3/4"-DIA. HOLE, 1" DEEP (BOTH SIDES)
C
1-1/2"
3/4"-DIA. HOLE
2-1/2"
A

DESK—FRONT DETAIL
BB
1-1/2"
3/16" FLAT
1/8" FLAT
W
B
CC
1-1/4"
1/8 x 18-1/4" SLOT, BEVEL BOTH SIDES
1-1/4"
1/4 x 3/8" RABBET
H

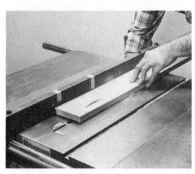

CUT THE DRAWING paper access slot by slowly raising the blade into the **work**. Tape on fence shows cutting limits.

USE SAME blind cut procedure to cut the opening for the swing-out tray. Use a sabre saw for the short end cuts.

USE A V-groove router bit to bevel paper slot edges. A wood block clamped to base accurately guides the router.

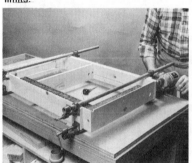

TABLE FRAME is dry-assembled, then clamped for boring screw pilot holes. Square is positioned to ensure accuracy.

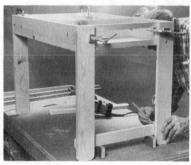

REASSEMBLE TABLE and bore screw holes in legs and stretchers. Mark the pieces to be shaped with corner-round bit.

INSERT HARDWOOD DOWELS in end grain to give hinge screws better holding power.

VIEW OF assembled table shows interior details prior to tabletop installation.

Assembly is with glue and screws. All screwheads are recessed (counterbored) and concealed with plugs cut from the same stock. Here's the best way to go about boring the screw holes: Use a 1/16-in.-dia. bit on the drill press to make straight holes in the front and rear aprons. Dry-assemble the ends and divider with bar clamps, then use the 1/16-in. bit with a portable drill to continue the holes into the mating pieces. Disassemble, then use the drill press to counterbore for the wood plugs and finally bore the screw shank holes. Before assembly, be sure to bore the holes for the roll paper dowel.

Glue-assemble the aprons and add the bottom panel, then clamp the legs and stretchers in place to repeat the screw-hole drilling sequence. Also mark the locations where stopped corner rounds must be made on the legs, aprons and stretchers. These cuts must be made with the router before final assembly, otherwise the router won't have full access to inside corners. The same procedure is followed for the chair.

The swing-out tray is made up of 1/2-in. stock and attached to a piece of 3/4-in. facing. The curved section is made by band-sawing a glued-up block, or it can be cut from a piece of 8/4

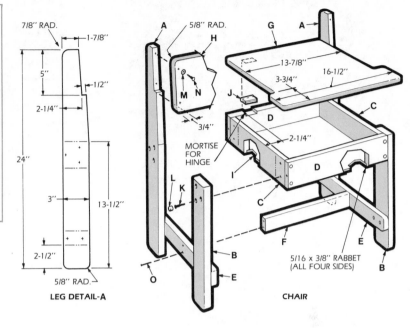

CHAIR

MATERIALS LIST

Key	No.	Size and description (use)
A	2	¾ x 3 x 24" pine (leg)
B	2	¾ x 3 x 13½" pine (leg)
C	2	¾ x 3 x 12½" pine (side)
D	2	¾ x 3 x 14" pine (end)
E	2	¾ x 1½ x 14" pine (stretcher)
F	1	¾ x 1½ x 12½" pine (stretcher)
G	1	½ x 14½ x 16½" MDO plywood (seat)
H	1	½ x 5½ x 17" MDO plywood (back)
I	1	¼ x 13¼ x 13¼" lauan plywood (bottom)
J	2	1¼ x 1½" butt hinge
K	20	1¼" No. 8 fh screws
L	20	⅜"-dia. wood plugs
M	4	No. 8 finish washers
N	4	1¼" No. 8 oval-head screws
O	*	1½" finishing nails
P	*	⅞" brads
Misc.:		Carpenter's glue
		* As required.

LEG DETAIL-A

7/8" RAD.
1-7/8"
5"
1/2"
2-1/4"
24"
3"
13-1/2"
2-1/2"
5/8" RAD.

CHAIR

5/8" RAD.
13-7/8"
16-1/2"
3-3/4"
2-1/4"
3/4"

MORTISE FOR HINGE

5/16 x 3/8" RABBET (ALL FOUR SIDES)

stock. Hardwood dowels are inserted in the hinge-screw locations where end grain is involved because end grain has poor screw-holding power. The short screws that come with the hinge are replaced by 1½-in. screws.

In order to bore the screw holes for this hinge in the table, you must use a chuck mounted on a flexible shaft due to the confined space.

The drawer case is assembled with butt joints, glue and 1½-in. finishing nails which are sunk and filled. Be sure to make the attaching ledge at the top overhang sufficiently so it locates under the divider piece in the table to facilitate solid screw attachment. When making the drawers, cut the finger cutouts before assembly.

The brackets for the tilting supports are homemade with four 3-in. flat corner plates. Two are bent to the right and two to the left. Use a dab of quick-setting epoxy to position the brackets on the blocks, as this will keep them in position for accurately boring the screw holes in the blocks. It most likely will be necessary to countersink the holes in the metal deeper to seat No. 8 flathead screws.

A note on hinging the seat: A double-depth mortise is cut into the apron only—the seat bottom is not mortised. The seat back needs no glue. It is secured with oval-head screws seated in finish (cup) washers. These hinges must be attached before installing the seat back or access to the screws will be impossible.

Applying the finish

For an easy-to-apply durable finish, use white primer followed with several coats of flat white. This was then top-coated with satin finish varnish. If you prefer, you can use glossy white and omit the clear satin.

The natural wood was given three light coats of clear satin finish varnish. *Important:* The second coat should be applied within one hour of the first; if the second coat is not completed in the first hour, wait at least 48 hours, or wrinkling of the first coat may occur. For best results, you should paint when the temperature is 70° to 80° F.

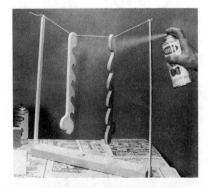

APPLY PRIMER and finish coats over the course of several light applications. Hang up the pieces to avoid messy handling.

Coat rack for a child

■ IF YOUR CHILDREN need a little help keeping their coats off the floor and their boots in one spot, this quick project is for you. Besides providing coat hooks at a height accessible to a child, it also incorporates a place to stow muddy boots by using a grocery carton as a disposable liner.

it also incorporates a place to stow muddy boots by using a grocery carton as a disposable liner.

Cut members to length from 1 x 4 clear pine or fir. Eliminate sharp corners from head-level by rounding off upright members with a sabre saw (see drawing). Cut the stub tenons on the base's side pieces with a backsaw. Then use a coping saw to remove the bulk of the waste from the two sockets in the front piece to match the tenons, finishing with a sharp chisel. Assemble unit with glue and flat head screws, countersinking them to prevent snags and tears. Sand well, and finish with stain and polyurethane, or enamel paint. Add coat hooks and corner braces to hold box.

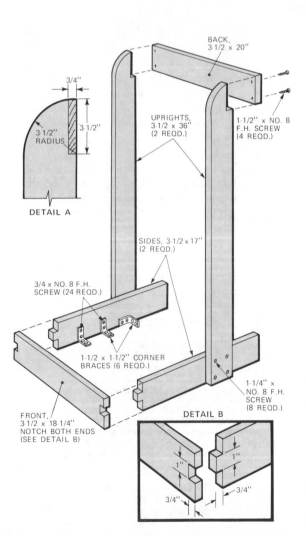

DETAIL A

3/4"

3-1/2" RADIUS

3-1/2"

BACK, 3-1/2 x 20"

UPRIGHTS, 3-1/2 x 36" (2 REQD.)

1-1/2" x NO. 8 F.H. SCREW (4 REQD.)

SIDES, 3-1/2 x 17" (2 REQD.)

3/4 x NO. 8 F.H. SCREW (24 REQD.)

1-1/2 x 1-1/2" CORNER BRACES (6 REQD.)

1-1/4" x NO. 8 F.H. SCREW (8 REQD.)

FRONT, 3-1/2 x 18-1/4" NOTCH BOTH ENDS (SEE DETAIL B)

DETAIL B

1"

1"

3/4"

3/4"

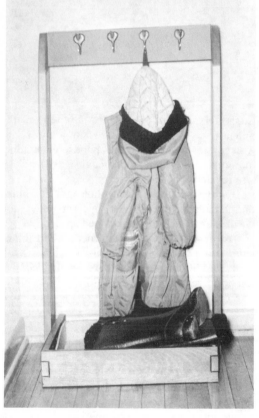

Rolltop desk for your youngster

■ THE ROLL-TOP LOOK of this desk is a great attraction for youngsters. Contrary to the real thing, though, this desktop simply swings up as a unit.

Materials used to build the desk are readily available. This one is built of 1-in pine (actually ¾-in thick). It is easy to work with and produces a neat appearance. Pine is less expensive than birch-veneered plywood and looks nicer than fir plywood.

The 16⅝x24⁷⁄₁₆-in. work surface (E) is made up of four pieces of 1-in. stock. Glue tongues of the short pieces into the grooves on the ends of the center boards. This joinery helps to prevent warping and assures that the board will slide between the guides. Keep the assembly clamped until the glue dries (at least overnight).

Cut the sides (C) and clamp them together and sand the edges smooth. Finish the sanding by hand, using 150-grit garnet paper on a sanding block.

Cut the remaining parts for the desk frame: the top (A), bottom trim (D), guides (F) and (G), braces (H), front (I) and filler (M). Cut the back (B) of ¼-in. plywood; cut the two pieces of ¾-in. half-round for the side trim.

Assemble the back and the sides of the desk frame. Use a temporary brace across the front to hold the assembly rigid while you apply bottom and side trim. Install the work-surface guides, checking for fit with work surface before applying glue. Add front rail (I). Then install corner braces to hold the unit square. Remove temporary brace.

To build the false tambour front, cut ends (J)

to shape and sand smooth. Fashioning the slat assembly is the time-consuming part of this project, unless you use the simplified procedure described later. I made the slats from two, 1-in.-thick, clear pine boards, each about 26 in. long.

Start by rounding all four edges of both pieces of pine stock. If you don't own a shaper, you can create the moldings using a router and rounding-over bit, or by hand with a block plane, rasp, surform tool and sandpaper.

Set the rip fence on your table saw to produce a ⅜-in. wide board and push the four edges through using a push stick. For minimum sanding, cut the moldings with a fine blade and use a slow feed.

To assemble slats to each other and to ends (J), temporarily tacknail a scrap piece of plywood to the back of the ends. Using a 1-in. brad as a drill bit, bore a hole near the center of each slat for nailing the adjacent slat. (*Editor's note:* Offset

these nailholes slightly on adjacent slats so that brads won't interfere with each other.) Run a *thin* line of glue between slats, being careful to avoid getting glue on the surface. Use a damp cloth to immediately wipe up glue squeezeout.

MATERIALS LIST— ROLL-TOP DESK

Key	No.	Size and description (use)
A	1	¾ x 9¼ x 27" pine (top)
B	1	¼ x 25¼ x 28" plywood (back)
C	2	¾ x 16 x 30" pine (side)
D	2	¾ x 3 x 16" pine (bottom trim)
E	1	¾ x 16⅜ x 24-7/16" pine (work surface)
F	2	¾ x ¾ x 15" pine (bottom guide)
G	2	¾ x ¾ x 11" pine (top guide)
H	2	¾ x 4½ x 4½" pine (brace)
I	1	¾ x 3½ x 24½" pine (front)
J	2	¾ x 8 x 9½" pine (end support)
K	1	⅜ x 1½ x 24⅜" pine (handle backing)
L	1	¼ x ⅜ x 3" pine (handle)
M	2	¼ x ⅜ x ⅜" pine (filler)

Misc.: ⅜"-dia: dowel, 1" clear pine about 26" long (or ¾" half-round pine molding) to make slats, 6d finishing nails, No. 16 x ¾" wire brads, 2 No. 10 x 1½" rh screws, 6 No. 8 x 1¼" rh screws, glue, sandpaper, stain, varnish.

HOW TO MAKE DESK TOP SLATS

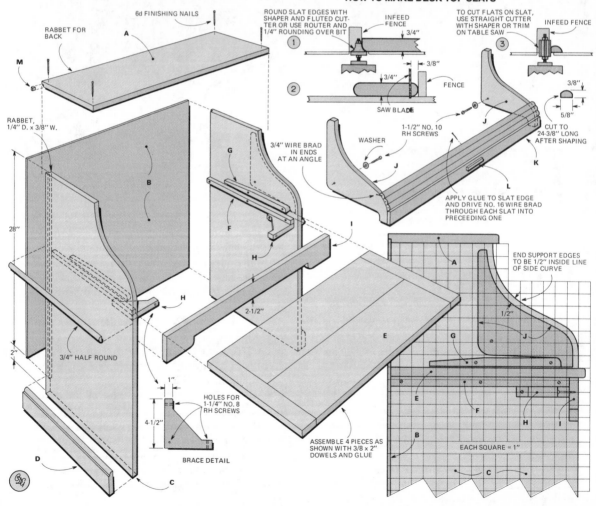

CLAMPING technique on wide pieces: C-clamps, boards prevent warping.

USE A 120-grit belt in sander to smooth contours of clamped sides.

TONGUE-AND-GROOVE joints are used on work surface (E).

APPLY GLUE sparingly to mating surfaces, wait 30 seconds, then assemble.

CLAMP BOARDS, using bar or pipe clamps; leave to dry overnight.

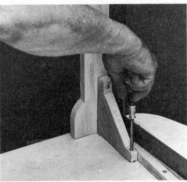

CORNER braces (H) are shop-made; install them using glue and screws.

CLEAR-PINE slat edges are rounded using shaper, router or block plane.

AFTER SHAPING slat edges, finish with 120-grit paper.

BORE SLIGHTLY offcenter hole in each slat using a 1-in. brad as bit. Run a thin glue line near back edge of slat.

BORE ANGLED pilot holes at ends, apply glue, set ¾-in. wire brads slightly. Temporary plywood back aids assembly.

Bore an angled hole at each end of each slat; use glue and ¾-in. brads to fasten slats to ends. Set the heads slightly. Use 1-in. nails at slat centers. An alternate, much simpler, procedure for making the roll-top front is to use ¾-in., half-round pine molding. But, the stain may "take" differently than on your pine case.

Building the chair

To prevent cracking, make the seat double thick, with ¾-in. pine (on top) and plywood framed by pine (bottom). Glue and clamp layers securely together. Make the pedestal from 1-in. iron floor flanges installed on 1x7-in. black-iron or galvanized pipe. Or use a standard 1x6-in. pipe nipple instead; it saves the cutting and threading charge. But base pieces (I) must then be cut 4½ in. high instead of 3½ in. Finish all parts before attaching pedestal. Paint metal with black enamel. Use primer on galvanized pipe and flanges.

Thoroughly sand all surfaces. Dust and wipe with a tack cloth. You can use a mellow pine stain followed by two coats of shellac.

MATERIALS LIST—CHILD'S DESK CHAIR

Key	No.	Size and description (use)
A	1	¾ × 12 × 14" (overall) pine (seat top)
B	1	¾ × 9½ × 11" (overall) plywood (seat bottom)
C	2	¾ × 1½ × length trimmed to fit, pine (seat-bottom edge)
D	1	¾ × 1 × length trimmed to fit, pine (seat-bottom edge)
E	1	¾ × 1½ × 9" (overall) pine (seat-bottom edge)
F	1	¾ × 10 × 12" pine (seat back)
G	2	¾ × 5 × 9" (overall) pine (arm support)
H	2	¾ × 1½ × 10" pine (arm)
I	2	1½ × 3½ × 15" (overall) pine, fir or spruce (base)*
J	2	1" iron floor flanges
K	1	1 × 7" black-iron or galvanized pipe*
L	11	No. 10 × 1½" fh screws
M	3	Wood plugs
N	20	No. 10 × 1¼" fh screws
O	as reqd.	6d finishing nails

Misc: White glue. *If a standard 1 × 6" nipple is used, cut 1½ × 4½ × 15" base pieces (I) from 2 × 6.

PINT-SIZED executive chair (above) consists of three basic assemblies—seat, pedestal and feet.

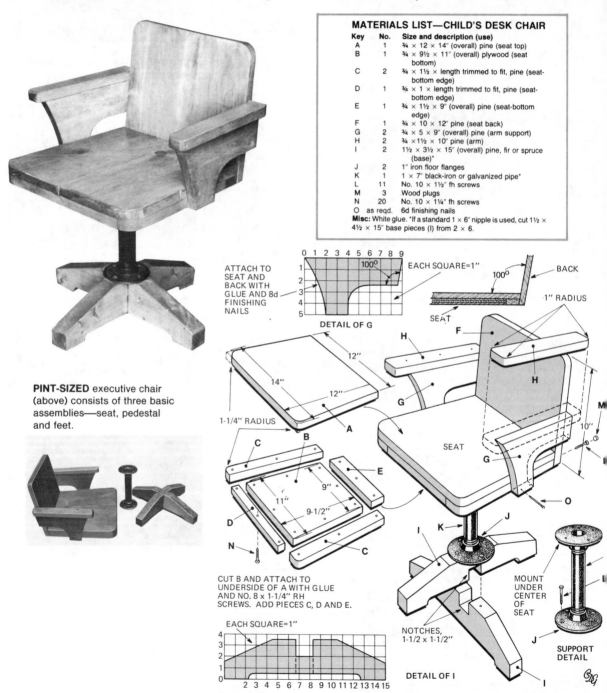

ATTACH TO SEAT AND BACK WITH GLUE AND 8d FINISHING NAILS

DETAIL OF G

EACH SQUARE=1"

100°

BACK

1" RADIUS

SEAT

12"

14"

12"

1-1/4" RADIUS

A

H

F

H

G

SEAT

G

M

10"

O

C

B

E

9"

11"

9-1/2"

D

C

N

I

K

J

CUT B AND ATTACH TO UNDERSIDE OF A WITH GLUE AND NO. 8 x 1-1/4" RH SCREWS. ADD PIECES C, D AND E.

EACH SQUARE=1"

DETAIL OF I

NOTCHES, 1-1/2 x 1-1/2"

MOUNT UNDER CENTER OF SEAT

J

SUPPORT DETAIL

I

This boy studies under his bed

■ NOT ONLY DOES this boy study under his bed, he sleeps over his desk. Far from being mixed up, he thinks he has the grooviest bunk bed/desk ever. This combination unit solves the space problem in a small room.

The two-in-one unit occupies a corner of the room from floor to ceiling to provide a regulation-size bunk bed and a kneehole desk with nearly a 4x7 ft. top. Ample in size for homework galore, the desk also presents a great hobby and play surface for model building, train and racing-car layouts—you name it. Three roomy drawers

flank each side of the kneehole with a pencil drawer above.

Constructed of common white pine, the unit is pretty much a duplicate each side of a centerline. Like members are made the same except for being assembled left and right hand. This is particularly true when making the four hollow posts and the two separate drawer compartments.

Since the posts butt against the ceiling, they have to be built in place. You can't expect to tip them up into place if put together on the floor. Each pair of end posts is joined with a panel of ¼-in. plywood, which can be plain or fancy with random grooves. If the bed is built in a corner, only the exposed end would require fancy plywood. If centered on a wall, both ends would be exposed. The distance between posts is set by the length of the steel bedrails. The original rails (and mattress) measure 75 in. long. They are for bunk beds without springs. After the rails are bolted to the posts of each end assembly, you can proceed to add the connecting board across the

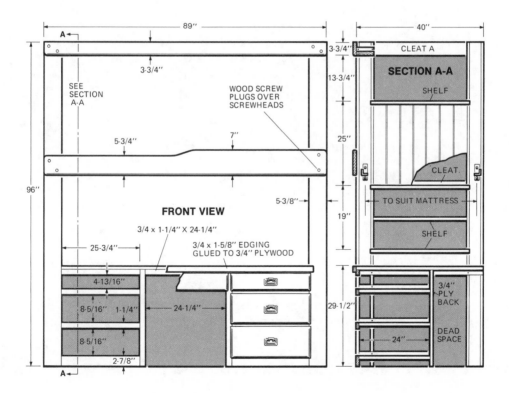

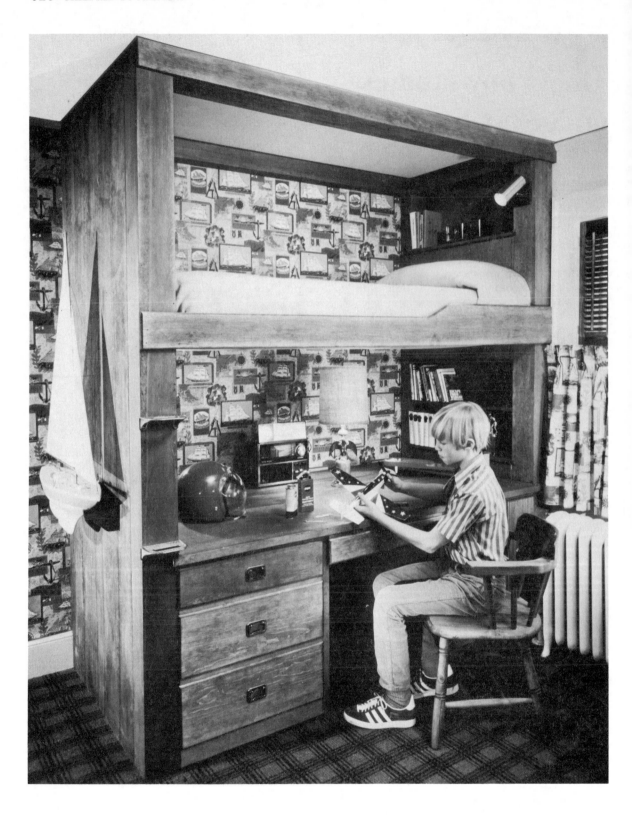

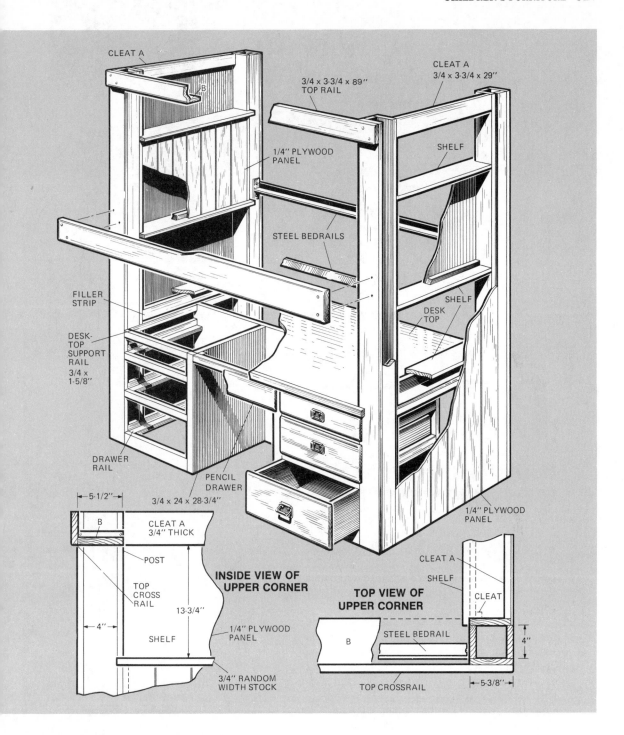

CLEAT A

B

CLEAT A
3/4 x 3-3/4 x 29"

3/4 x 3-3/4 x 89"
TOP RAIL

1/4" PLYWOOD
PANEL

SHELF

STEEL BEDRAILS

SHELF

FILLER
STRIP

DESK-
TOP
SUPPORT
RAIL
3/4 x
1-5/8"

DESK
TOP

DRAWER
RAIL

PENCIL
DRAWER
3/4 x 24 x 28-3/4"

1/4" PLYWOOD
PANEL

5-1/2"

B

CLEAT A
3/4" THICK

POST

TOP
CROSS
RAIL

4"

SHELF

13-3/4"

**INSIDE VIEW OF
UPPER CORNER**

1/4" PLYWOOD
PANEL

3/4" RANDOM
WIDTH STOCK

CLEAT A

SHELF

CLEAT

**TOP VIEW OF
UPPER CORNER**

B

STEEL BEDRAIL

4"

TOP CROSSRAIL

5-3/8"

top at the ceiling and the board that hides the bed rail. These are fastened with screws set in counterbored holes and capped with plugs.

The rails of the drawer compartments are attached to the front posts with dowels. Notice that a full-length plywood panel provides a back for each compartment and the kneehole. This panel also supports the outside drawer slides at the rear.

Make any minor adjustments to the dimensions to fit your particular situation. When construction is complete, the unit is ready for finishing to match the decor of the room.

Bunk bed with a built-in chest

■ NO NEED TO WORRY about getting this king-size bunk bed in and out of the room; it all comes apart with a twist of a screwdriver, thanks to special hardware connectors holding the 14 parts together.

The bed makes the most of space—four large drawers built in under the mattress swallow up lots of toys, extra blankets, sheets and pillow cases. Two "ladder" shelves at the foot of the bed provide still more storage space, and another shelf across the headboard will hold a lot of bedtime-story books. The bed accommodates a 36 x 75-in. foam-rubber mattress. The complete bed is built from ¾-in. fir plywood. Half-round molding covers the exposed edges of the sides.

The two-part connectors consist of a steel pin with a large head and a slotted 1-in. steel disc installed in the line with the pin. When the disc engages the pin and is turned with a screwdriver, it draws the joint tight. You'll need 28 connectors called Elite 25 with DU91 dowel.

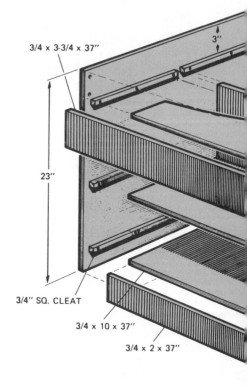

3/4 x 3-3/4 x 37"

3"

23"

3/4" SQ. CLEAT

3/4 x 10 x 37"

3/4 x 2 x 37"

Technical Art by Peter Trojan

CLEATS SUPPORT plywood top where the mattress rests. They're glued and screwed 3 inches from the top.

DRAWERS ROLL smoothly on standard metal guides which are screwed to the dividers and the drawer sides.

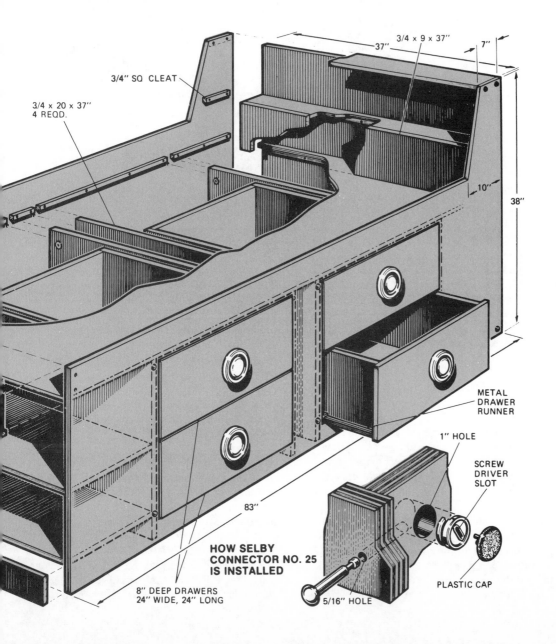

3/4" SQ CLEAT

3/4 x 20 x 37"
4 REQD.

3/4 x 9 x 37"

37"

7"

10"

38"

METAL
DRAWER
RUNNER

1" HOLE

SCREW
DRIVER
SLOT

83"

**HOW SELBY
CONNECTOR NO. 25
IS INSTALLED**

8" DEEP DRAWERS
24" WIDE, 24" LONG

5/16" HOLE

PLASTIC CAP

Heirloom cradle

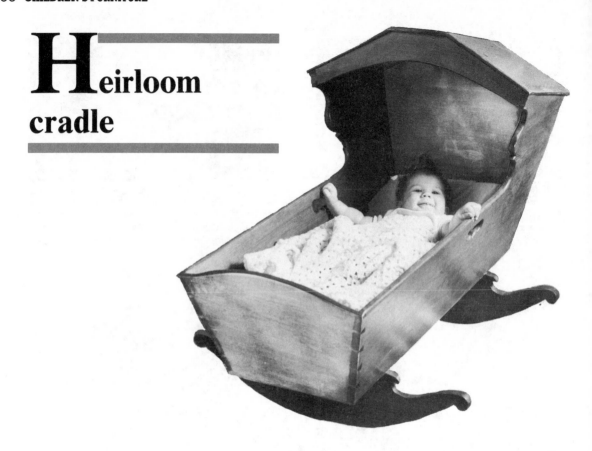

■ THE CRADLE SHOWN here used pieces of rough-sawn eastern white pine, planed to the following thicknesses: ⅝ in. for the sides and ends; ⅞ in. for the rockers, stretchers and bottom; ⁵⁄₁₆ in. for the hood. You could use 1-in. planed commercial lumber as is for the thicker parts, and planed stock for the thinner ones. The native pine selected was used in the original cradles, but cherry, walnut or other native woods were also used by colonial craftsmen.

The next step is to make full-size patterns on cardboard or kraft paper. Use the patterns given here as a guide. Cut only the sides, foot and head ends at this time. The patterns for the pieces containing curved parts are placed on a grid. Draw a grid of 1-in. squares on the pattern paper. Use a sharp pencil aided by a straightedge to draw the straight lines of each part. Sketch in the contoured lines.

Lay the patterns on the lumber, considering the direction of the grain and interesting markings. You can glue up lumber for the head end with carpenter's glue. Then plane the glue line and sand the piece with 80-grit abrasive.

Use a dovetail saw and wood chisel to make the dovetail joints. First, lay out a practice set of dovetails on stock the same thickness as the cradle stock. Determine the number of pins needed. The cradle shown uses a 2-in. on-center spacing, but adjusted enough to have one pin at the top and another at the bottom of each joint. Lay out the practice board for the pins first. Then use the other board as a gauge to determine the depth of the pins. Make a light pencil line on both sides of the board to indicate this depth.

Use dividers set to measure the centers for the pins. Mark all pin centers in on both sides of the board. Use a try square to extend these marks into centerlines.

You can make the pins ¼ in. wide on the inside and taper them to ¹⁄₁₆ in. on the outside. Work from the centerlines with dividers to determine the width of the pins on both sides of the wood. Then pencil in the pin outlines on both sides and board ends, using a try square and straightedge.

Cutting the dovetails

Before you cut the pins, be sure your tools are truly sharp. Then put the board in the vise, the end with the pins upward. Cut the edge of the pins with the dovetail saw. Lay the board on the bench and cut between the pins, using wide wood chisels. Cut both sides toward the center.

Lay out the tails by placing a practice board (representing the cradle side) on the bench and holding the piece with pins on it in a vertical position. Outline the pins carefully with a sharp pencil. Straighten the tracings with the aid of a straightedge. Then cut the tails with a dovetail saw and chisel. After you cut these out, try fitting the parts together. A tight fit is better than a loose one.

A sharp pocketknife or fine rasp can be used to remove extra wood a little at a time. Once you have a practice set of dovetails that suits you, proceed with the cradle. There are only nine pins on each side of the head, six pins on each side of the foot and one on each side of the hooded front. The top and bottom pins at each end of the joints are actually only part of a pin.

Assembling the cradle

You can make the handholes in the sides by boring two 1-in.-dia. holes and connecting them with a decorative cut. Assemble the sides and ends dry, in order to take final measurements for the bottom and hood front. Set a sliding T-bevel on the inside of the assembly to determine the angle for the bottom. Cut the bottom to size.

Round the top edges and handhole edges with a ⅜-in. rounding-over bit in a router. Don't extend these cuts into the dovetail corners. Round these corners by hand after assembly. Cut the front of the hood to fit properly between the sides. Then cut the single pin in the center of each end, and cut the matching tails in the sides. Assemble parts with glue.

To ensure uniform rockers, begin by drawing only half the pattern on stiff paper. Fold the paper and cut it so a full rocker is revealed when the paper is unfolded. Cut out both rockers at the same time on a band saw, by piggybacking the wood blanks and nailing them together through the waste.

Cut the template for the stretcher in a manner similar to the rocker template. Cut dadoes ¼ in. into the rockers to accept the ends of the stretcher. Ease the cradle sides where they come in contact with the rockers. Assemble the rockers and stretcher to the cradle, using 1¾-in. No. 10 flathead screws and glue. Use two screws in each rocker and three in the stretcher. Counterbore and plug the screwholes.

Cut out the top of the hood. Temporarily nail it in place. Measure and cut the side pieces, being sure to get the correct angle. Round the outside

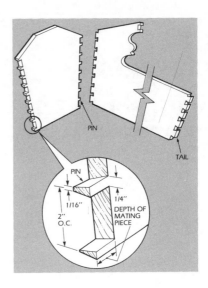

edges with sandpaper and assemble the hood with glue and fine ¾-in. brads set and covered with wood filler.

Sanding and finishing

After cleaning off pencil marks and surface dirt with a solvent cleaner, hand-sand the cradle and finish. Stain the wood cherry and apply two coats of antique varnish. Upholstery foam 2 in. thick covered with a plastic shower curtain makes a good pad for the cradle.

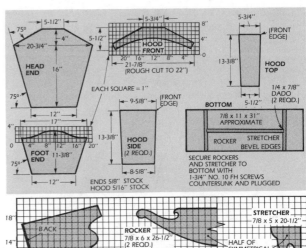

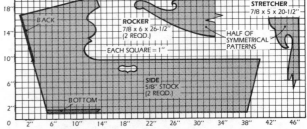

Playcubes— easy as 1, 2, 3

■ THESE ATTRACTIVE storage seats offer a partial remedy to the where-to-put-it problem by concealing many odds and ends. Topped with fabric-covered foam rubber, they also serve as extra seating when needed.

Each of the cubes has a numeral graphic on its side. You might build a cube featuring your youngster's age or initial.

The basic box is constructed of 1x12-in. clear pine with a plywood bottom and top. Begin work on the cube by cutting the side panels (A, see drawing) with mitered sides. Plow dadoes to accept the top cleats (E) and cut rabbets for bottom (C).

Next, use a table saw to cut grooves for the splines (D). Shape the numeral on the side panel with a router and straight cutter. To do it, first make a template of ⅛-in. hardboard using a numeral on the facing page. The finished numerals are 9¾ in. high. However, the template must be larger to allow for the difference between the bearing and the cutter diameter. Use a ¼-in. straight mortising bit and a ⁷⁄₁₆-in. router template guide, so the template is ³⁄₃₂-in. larger all around than the finished numeral.

Rout the numeral

Clamp the template rigidly to a side panel. Adjust the router so its cutter will rout the numeral to a ⅜-in. depth *in the side panel*. Remove

CREATE A TEMPLATE out of ⅛-in. hardboard that will suit your router shoe (see text). Clamp it to the workpiece for routing the numerals or letters.

SINCE ROUTER cutter leaves rounded corners, you will need to use a chisel and hammer to make the square shapes. Then sand the cutout.

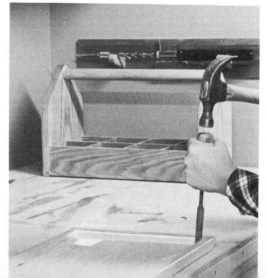

the template and chisel corners square.

After cutting the bottom (C) and the corner splines (D), assemble the box with glue and clamps. Set it aside to dry. The next day, beef up joint strength by using 6d finishing nails spaced 6 in. apart on alternate sides of the miter joint. Set the nails. Cut top cleats (E) and base (F) and glue parts in place. Cut the wood top (B) so it fits loosely and removes easily for access. Bore a ¾-in.-dia. finger hole at the center.

Apply wood filler as needed and sand the cube with 120-grit abrasive paper. Dust and wipe with a tack cloth. Brush on two coats of 3-lb. cut white shellac, the first coat thinned 50 percent with denatured alcohol, the second coat brushed on as it comes from the can. If desired, paint the numeral.

Cut out a cushion of 2-in.-thick foam rubber. Sew a suitable fabric slipcover to complement the cube.

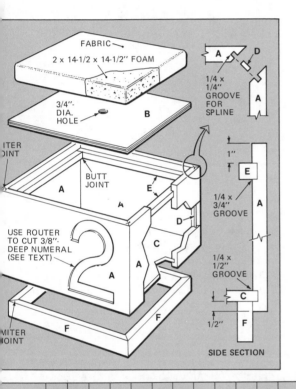

MATERIALS LIST—PLAYCUBE

Key	No.	Size and description (use)
A	4	¾ × 11¼ × 16" clear pine (side panels)
B	1	⅜ × 14⅜ × 14⅜" plywood (seat top)
C	1	½ × 15 × 15" plywood (bottom)
D	4	¼ × ½ × 11¼" plywood (splines)
E	4	¾ × 1 × 14" pine (top cleats)
F	4	¾ × 2 × 14½" pine (base strips)

Misc.: White glue, ⅛" hardboard for template, 6d finishing nails, wood filler, 3-lb. cut shellac, prime coat, paint, cushion fabric and 2 × 14½ × 14½" foam rubber.

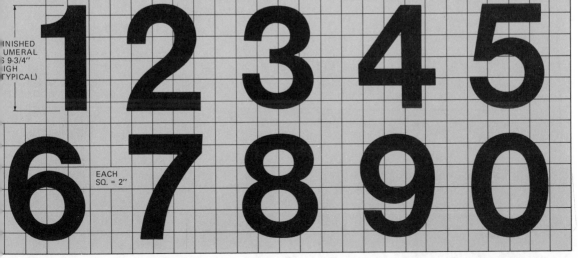

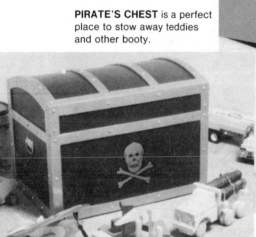

PIRATE'S CHEST is a perfect place to stow away teddies and other booty.

ALPHABET BOX: A personalized trunk may give your child incentive to keep the room in top shape. It's a good way to show a toddler how to keep all her toys organized in one spot.

Toyboxes please everyone

■ YOUR CHILD will learn that getting organized can be a pleasure with a handy toybox to help. By following this basic design, you can make a toybox or storage chest with one sheet of plywood; then finish it with one of four decorative touches. Choose a design to match the setting.

STAGECOACH TRUNK: Here's a rugged-looking trunk that is handsome enough to grace your family room.

PENNSYLVANIA DUTCH blanket chest: A touch of decoration turns our basic box into a dainty storage place for fabric and yarn in the sewing room.

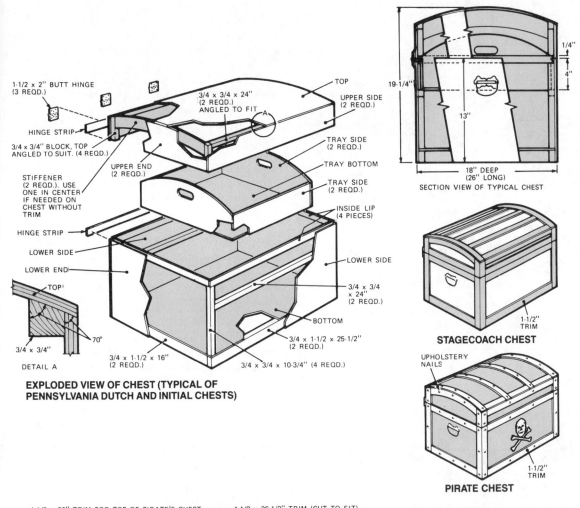

1-1/2 x 2" BUTT HINGE (3 REQD.)

HINGE STRIP

3/4 x 3/4" BLOCK, TOP ANGLED TO SUIT. (4 REQD.)

STIFFENER (2 REQD.). USE ONE IN CENTER IF NEEDED ON CHEST WITHOUT TRIM

HINGE STRIP

LOWER SIDE

LOWER END

TOP:

3/4 x 3/4"   70°

DETAIL A

3/4 x 3/4 x 24" (2 REQD.) ANGLED TO FIT

UPPER END (2 REQD.)

A

3/4 x 1-1/2 x 16" (2 REQD.)

3/4 x 3/4 x 10-3/4" (4 REQD.)

3/4 x 1-1/2 x 25-1/2" (2 REQD.)

BOTTOM

3/4 x 3/4 x 24" (2 REQD.)

LOWER SIDE

INSIDE LIP (4 PIECES)

TRAY SIDE (2 REQD.)

TRAY BOTTOM

TRAY SIDE (2 REQD.)

TOP

UPPER SIDE (2 REQD.)

EXPLODED VIEW OF CHEST (TYPICAL OF PENNSYLVANIA DUTCH AND INITIAL CHESTS)

19-1/4"   13"   1/4"   4"

18" DEEP (26" LONG)

SECTION VIEW OF TYPICAL CHEST

STAGECOACH CHEST

1-1/2" TRIM

UPHOLSTERY NAILS

PIRATE CHEST

1-1/2" TRIM

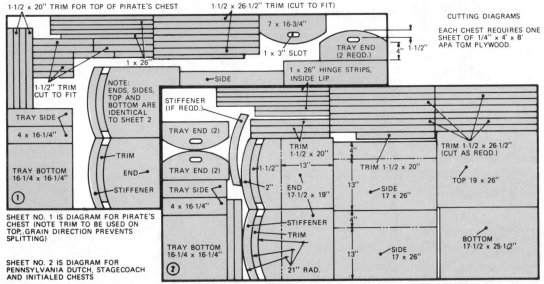

1-1/2 x 20" TRIM FOR TOP OF PIRATE'S CHEST

1-1/2 x 26-1/2" TRIM (CUT TO FIT)

7 x 16-3/4"

1 x 3" SLOT

1 x 26"

1-1/2" TRIM CUT TO FIT

TRAY SIDE

4 x 16-1/4"

TRAY BOTTOM 16-1/4 x 16-1/4"

①

NOTE: ENDS, SIDES, TOP AND BOTTOM ARE IDENTICAL TO SHEET 2

TRAY END (2)

TRAY END (2)

TRAY SIDE

4 x 16-1/4"

TRAY BOTTOM 16-1/4 x 16-1/4"

②

TRIM

END

STIFFENER

STIFFENER (IF REQD.)

1 x 26" HINGE STRIPS, INSIDE LIP

SIDE

TRAY END (2 REQD.)

4"   1-1/2"

TRIM 1-1/2 x 20"

1-1/2"   13"

2"

END 17-1/2 x 19"

STIFFENER

TRIM

21" RAD.

TRIM 1-1/2 x 20"

SIDE 17 x 26"

13"

SIDE 17 x 26"

13"

TRIM 1-1/2 x 26-1/2" (CUT AS REQD.)

TOP 19 x 26"

BOTTOM 17-1/2 x 25-1/2"

CUTTING DIAGRAMS

EACH CHEST REQUIRES ONE SHEET OF 1/4" x 4' x 8' APA TGM PLYWOOD.

SHEET NO. 1 IS DIAGRAM FOR PIRATE'S CHEST (NOTE TRIM TO BE USED ON TOP, GRAIN DIRECTION PREVENTS SPLITTING)

SHEET NO. 2 IS DIAGRAM FOR PENNSYLVANIA DUTCH, STAGECOACH AND INITIALED CHESTS

The toybox designs can be built inexpensively. All you need for each chest is a single sheet of ¼-in. A-B plywood, some 1 x 1 and 1 x 2 pine to frame the box, carpenter's glue, paint and simple hardware.

The boxes have a 4-in.-deep, 16-in.-square tray with cut-out handles for lift-out storage of special small toys and supplies.

If you make the pirate's chest, you'll want to add gold-painted trim pieces cut from scrap plywood, brass upholstery tacks and a skull and crossbones. Use a wood-graining kit to give the stagecoach box an oldtime look. Then add trim and two handles to make heaving the trunk on the coach a little easier.

To make the Pennsylvania Dutch design, draw the pattern shown and cut a stencil on heavy paper. Or, trace the design on the box in soft pencil; then paint it freehand. The alphabet toybox is easy to paint by using masking tape to mask off the letters.

Note: When making any furniture for children, be sure to use special safety hinges and other hardware designed to prevent accidents.

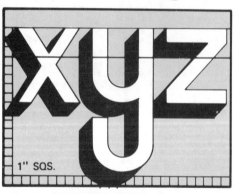

INITIALED CHEST

PIRATE'S CHEST

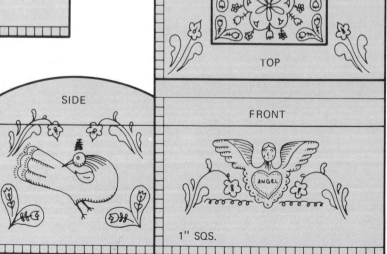

PENNSYLVANIA DUTCH CHEST

Projects for the children's room

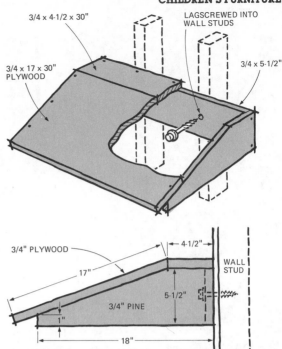

3/4 x 4-1/2 x 30"

3/4 x 17 x 30" PLYWOOD

LAGSCREWED INTO WALL STUDS

3/4 x 5-1/2"

3/4" PLYWOOD

4-1/2"

17"

WALL STUD

5-1/2"

3/4" PINE

1"

18"

SIDE VIEW

■ ONE THING ABOUT children's furniture—it's usually simple to make, and that goes for this novel wall-hung desk and footboard bed table. Both require little more than a hammer and saw to build. You simply saw the pieces to size, apply glue, nail together, paint and you're through. The job is even simpler if you have your lumber dealer do the cutting for a small extra charge.

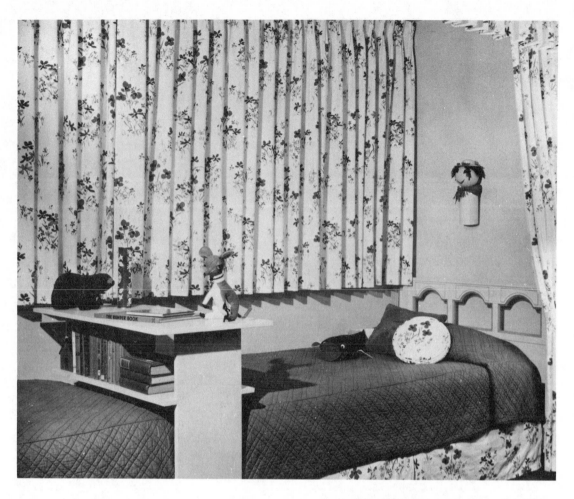

The wall-hung desk becomes plenty strong to work on when it's anchored to wall studs with a couple of husky lagscrews, and there's nothing underneath to bang knees on or interfere with cleaning. A good height from the floor is about 30 in. The desktop is slightly sloped for easier reading, writing and sketching. The footboard table is made to straddle twin beds placed end to end along a wall. To change the bedding, you just lift the table out of the way.

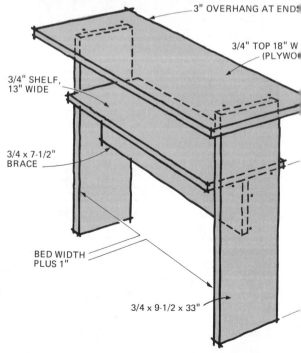

3" OVERHANG AT ENDS

3/4" TOP 18" W (PLYWO

3/4" SHELF, 13" WIDE

3/4 x 7-1/2" BRACE

BED WIDTH PLUS 1"

3/4 x 9-1/2 x 33"

CUSTOMARY TO METRIC (CONVERSION)

Conversion factors can be carried so far they become impractical. In cases below where an entry is exact it is followed by an asterisk (*). Where considerable rounding off has taken place, the entry is followed by a + or a − sign.

Linear Measure

inches	millimeters
1/16	1.5875*
1/8	3.2
3/16	4.8
1/4	6.35*
5/16	7.9
3/8	9.5
7/16	11.1
1/2	12.7*
9/16	14.3
5/8	15.9
11/16	17.5
3/4	19.05*
13/16	20.6
7/8	22.2
15/16	23.8
1	25.4*

inches	centimeters
1	2.54*
2	5.1
3	7.6
4	10.2
5	12.7*
6	15.2
7	17.8
8	20.3
9	22.9
10	25.4*
11	27.9
12	30.5

feet	centimeters	meters
1	30.48*	.3048*
2	61	.61
3	91	.91
4	122	1.22
5	152	1.52
6	183	1.83
7	213	2.13
8	244	2.44
9	274	2.74
10	305	3.05
50	1524*	15.24*
100	3048*	30.48*

1 yard = .9144* meters
1 rod = 5.0292* meters
1 mile = 1.6 kilometers
1 nautical mile = 1.852* kilometers

Weights

ounces	grams
1	28.3
2	56.7
3	85
4	113
5	142
6	170
7	198
8	227
9	255
10	283
11	312
12	340
13	369
14	397
15	425
16	454

Formula (exact):
ounces × 28.349 523 125* = grams

pounds	kilograms
1	.45
2	.9
3	1.4
4	1.8
5	2.3
6	2.7
7	3.2
8	3.6
9	4.1
10	4.5

1 short ton (2000 lbs) = 907 kilograms (kg)
Formula (exact):
pounds × .453 592 37* = kilograms

Miscellaneous

1 British thermal unit (Btu) (mean)
  = 1 055.9 joules
1 horsepower = 745.7 watts
    = .75 kilowatts
caliber (diameter of a firearm's
  bore in hundredths of an inch)
  = .254 millimeters (mm)

1 atmosphere pressure = 101 325*
  pascals (newtons per sq meter)
1 pound per square inch (psi) =
  6 895 pascals
1 pound per square foot =
  47.9 pascals
1 knot = 1.85 kilometers per hour
1 mile per hour = 1.6093
  kilometers per hour

Fluid Measure

(Milliliters [ml] and cubic centimeters [cc] are equivalent, but it is customary to use milliliters for liquids.)

1 cu in	=	16.39 ml
1 fl oz	=	29.6 ml
1 cup	=	237 ml
1 pint	=	473 ml
1 quart	=	946 ml
	=	.946 liters
1 gallon	=	3785 ml
	=	3.785 liters

Formula (exact):
fluid ounces × 29.573 529 562 5*
  = milliliters

Volume

1 cu in	=	16.39 cubic centimeters (cc)
1 cu ft	=	28 316.7 cc
1 bushel	=	35 239.1 cc
1 peck	=	8 809.8 cc

Area

1 sq in	=	6.45 sq cm
1 sq ft	=	929 sq cm
	=	.093 sq meters
1 sq yd	=	.84 sq meters
1 acre	=	4 046.9 sq meters
	=	.404 7 hectares
1 sq mile	=	2 589 988 sq meters
	=	259 hectares
	=	2.589 9 sq kilometers